James Martineau:

"This Conscience-Intoxicated Unitarian"

James Martineau: "This Conscience-Intoxicated Unitarian." © 2002 by Frank Schulman. Printed and bound in the United States of America. No part of this book may be reproduced in any form or by any electronic or mechanical means including information storage and retrieval systems without written permission from the publisher, except by a reviewer, who may quote brief passages in a review. Published by Meadville Lombard Theological School Press, 5701 S. Woodlawn Avenue, Chicago, Illinois 60637. First Edition.

ISBN: 0-9702479-1-5

Editing, design, and layout by Laura Horton

James Martineau: "This Conscience-Intoxicated Unitarian"

by

Frank Schulman

James Martineau

Table of Contents

Chronology of Martineau's Life ix

Introduction 1

Chapter I: Biography and Influences 5
   1. Martineau's Life 5
   2. Martineau's Character 7
   3. Influences 10

Chapter II: Martineau's Theory of Worship 15
   1. Overview 15
   2. The Nature and Purpose of Worship 19
   3. Martineau's Prayer Book 24
   4. Rites 29
      A. Baptism and Christening 29
      B. Communion 32
   5. Elements of Worship 35
      A. Hymns 35
          A Collection of Hymns for Christian Worship ... 37
          Hymns for the Christian Church and Home 38
          Hymns of Praise and Prayer 39
      B. Prayer 41
      C. Sermons 44

Table of Contents

Chapter III: Martineau's Concept of the Ministry 55

   1. The Nature of the Ministry 55
   2. The Role of the Minister 60
   3. The Need for a Learned Ministry 63
   4. Martineau's Advice to Ministers 67

Chapter IV: Martineau's Sources of Authority 73

   1. Reason 77
      A. The Supremacy of Reason 77
      B. The Limits of Reason 79
   2. The Bible 81
      A. The Older Belief 81
      B. Biblical Criticism 83
      C. Against Biblical Literalism 84
      D. The Importance of the Bible 87
   3. Tradition 88
      A. Christ as Authority 89
      B. Is Christianity the Superior Way? 90
   4. The Moral Law 93
      A. The Moral Law and Its Consequences 93
      B. The Moral Law as Intuition 95
      C. The Moral Law as Absolute 98
   5. Conscience 100
      A. Conscience as the Key to Religion 100
      B. The Authority of Conscience 103
      C. Conscience as the Voice of God 104

Chapter V. Martineau's Theology 109

   1. God 109
      A. An Outline of Martineau's Thought 109
      B. Science and God 111
      C. How God Is Revealed 113
      D. The Personal God 114
      E. Duty 118
   2. Human Nature 119
      A. The Human as Incarnation 119

    B. Temptations 121
    C. Suffering 123
    D. The Dual Nature of Humanity 124
  3. Jesus 126
    A. Martineau's Christology 126
    B. The Nature of Jesus 128
    C. The Religion of, Not about, Jesus 130
    D. What Jesus Taught 132
  4. Ecclesiology 134
    A. Defining the Church 135
    B. The Church as Community 139
    C. The Decline of Christianity after the Apostles 142
    D. What Is a Christian? 144
    E. Martineau's Understanding of Christianity 148
  5. The Hope of Immortality 149
    A. The Meaning of Death 149
    B. The Nature of Immortality 151
    C. The Assurance of Immortality 153
    D. Future Salvation 154

Chapter VI. Conclusion 161

Bibliography 163

Chronology of Martineau's Life

1805   April 21: Martineau is born in Magdalen St., Norwich, youngest of seven children of Thomas (d. June 21, 1826) and Elizabeth (b. 1770, d. Aug 26, 1848) Martineau.

1815   Martineau is sent to Norwich grammar school.

1819   Martineau is sent to boarding school of Lant Carpenter.

1821   Martineau is apprenticed to Samuel Fox of Derby to become a civil engineer; he boards with Edward Higginson, Unitarian minister, whose daughter Helen he later married.

1822   Jan. 31: Henry Turner, Unitarian minister in Nottingham, dies at 29; Martineau determined to become Unitarian minister.

1822   Sept. 22: Martineau enters Manchester College York, where he is taught by Charles Wellbeloved, John Kenrick, and William Turner; he wins high honors.

1824   June 3: Martineau's oldest brother Thomas dies at age 29.

Martineau delivers the oration "The Necessity of Cultivating the Imagination as a Regulator of the Devotional Feelings."

1826   Martineau's father dies.

1827   Martineau finishes college.

1827   July 4: Martineau preaches the annual sermon at Easter Union Associationn., Halesworth, in Suffolk.

1827   August 1: Martineau becomes assistant to Lant Carpenter, Bristol.

1828	Sept. 28: Martineau is appointed co-pastor with Philip Taylor, Eustace Street, Dublin.
1828	Oct. 26: Martineau is ordained by Dublin Presbytery, Synod of Munster.
	Dec. 18: Martineau marries Helen Higginson, the daughter of Rev. Edward Higginson of Derby.
1829	Birth of Martineau's daughter Helen (d. 1830).
	March: Martineau participates in the formation of the Irish Unitarian Christian Society in Dublin, acting as secretary.
1831	Birth of Martineau's son Russell (d. 1898).
1831	Martineau's first hymnal, *A Collection of Hymns for Christian Worship*, is published in Dublin.
1831	Martineau's Dublin ministry is highly appreciated by his congregation, though his profession of the humanity of Christ provokes controversy.
1831	Sept. 27: death of Philip Taylor. Martineau succeeds to a share of the regium donum and resigns on Oct. 31 rather than accepting it.
1831	Nov. 13: Martineau's Dublin congregation accepts his resignation in a close vote.
1832	Birth of Martineau's daughter Isabella (d. 1900).
1832	July 1: Martineau becomes the co-pastor of Paradise Street Chapel, Liverpool, with John Grundy.
1833	Birth of Martineau's daughter Mary (d. 1902).
1835	Birth of Martineau's son Herbert (d. 1846).
1835	Jan. 28: Grundy resigns, leaving Martineau as sole pastor of Paradise Street Chapel.
1835	Martineau writes for *The London Review*.
1835	Aug. 14: Martineau's son Herbert is born.
1836	Martineau helps to found Liverpool Domestic Mission.
1836	*Rationale of Religious Enquiry*.

1837	Birth of Martineau's daughter Gertrude (d. 1924).
1838	Martineau writes for *Christian Teacher*.
1839	Birth of Martineau's son Basil (d. 1906).
1839	The Liverpool Controversy.
1840	*Hymns for the Christian Church and Home*.
1840	Oct.: Martineau becomes Professor of Mental and Moral Philosophy and Political Economy at Manchester New College (Manchester).
1842	Birth of Martineau's daughter Edith (d. 1909).
1843	*Endeavours After the Christian Life*.
1845–54	Martineau becomes editor (with Charles Wicksteed) of *Prospective Review* and its successor, *National Review* (1855–64). He occasionally helps to edit *Theological Review*.
1845	July: Martineau's sermon "The Bible and the Child" leads to a break with Biblical conservatives within Unitarianism.
1846	March 28: Martineau's son Herbert dies.
1847	*Endeavours, Second Series*.
1848	Martineau's mother dies.
1848	July 16: Paradise Street Church is to be rebuilt in Hope Street (Liverpool). Martineau delivers his farewell sermon "Pause and Retrospect" and goes to Germany for 15 months of study.
1851	March: Martineau breaks with his sister, Harriet, over her review of *Letters on the Laws of Man's Nature and Development*, by Henry George Atkinson.
1853	Manchester College moves to London. Martineau travels from Liverpool to London to lecture every week for five years.
1856	April 4: Martineau resigns from Hope Street Chapel.
1857	Feb. 20: Martineau's resignation from Hope Street Chapel is accepted.
1858	*Studies of Christianity*.
1858–68	Martineau serves as a trustee of Dr. Williams' Trust.

1859	Feb. 20: Martineau begins a co-ministry at Little Portland Street Chapel, London, with John James Tayler.
1860	Martineau becomes sole minister of Little Portland Street Church.
1866	Martineau applies for the chair of mental philosophy and logic at University College London but is turned down because he is a cleric. Faculty protests ensue.
1868	Martineau helps to form the Free Christian Union.
1869	Jan. 2: Martineau joins the Metaphysical Society, founded by Lord Tennyson, where he remains a member until 1880.
1869	Martineau becomes Principal of Manchester New College on the death of John James Tayler.
1872	June 26: Martineau is awarded an honorary LL.D. by Harvard University.
1872	Oct. 16: Martineau resigns from Little Portland Street Chapel because of illness.
1873	*Hymns of Praise and Prayer*.
1875	Feb. 8: Martineau is awarded an honorary S.Th.D. by the University of Leyden.
1875	*Hours of Thought on Sacred Things*.
1877	Martineau's wife Helen dies.
1879	*Hours of Thought on Sacred Things, Second Series*.
1882	*Study of Spinoza*.
1884	April 17: Martineau is awarded an honorary D.D. by the University of Edinburgh.
1884	Martineau writes the introduction to E. P. Hall's translation of Bonet-Maury's *Early Sources of English Unitarian Christianity*.
1885	Martineau resigns as principal of Manchester New College.
1885	*Types of Ethical Theory*, 2 vols.
1886–87	Martineau serves as president of Manchester New College.

1888	June 20: Martineau is awarded a D.C.L. Honoris Causa by Oxford University.
1888	Martineau introduces plans for the organization of Unitarians as "English Presbyterians."
1889	Martineau opposes the move of Manchester College to Oxford.
1889	Oct. 19: Martineau conducts communion on the opening of Manchester College Oxford.
1890	*The Seat of Authority in Religion.*
1890–91	*Essays, Reviews and Addresses*, 4 vols.
1891	Jan.–Mar: Martineau lectures at University Hall, Gordon Square, on the Gospel of Luke and the newly discovered Gospel According to Peter.
1891	*Home Prayers, With Two Services for Public Worship.*
1892	July 8: Martineau is awarded an honorary Litt. D. by Dublin University.
1897	*Faith the Beginning, Self-Surrender the Fulfilment, of the Spiritual Life.*
1898	Jan.: Martineau's sermon "The Constancy of Nature and the Faithfulness of God" published in *The Inquirer*.
1898	Oct. 18: A statue of Martineau is unveiled in the library of Manchester College.
1900	Jan. 11: Martineau dies at 35 Gordon Square, London.

Introduction

The prominent English theologian James Martineau (1805–1900), who, according to J. B. Schneewind, was the greatest leader of the Unitarians in Victorian England,[1] spent his productive years as a minister, a teacher, and the principal of Manchester College, where he was responsible for the training of ministerial students. He published five volumes of sermons, a prayer book, three hymnals, and major works of theology and philosophy. Influential in the Unitarian movement, Martineau had a considerable impact on the religious thought of England. He published significant works on the sources of authority for religion and ethics; four volumes of essays, reviews, and addresses; and several other books.

This book attempts to outline James Martineau's ideas on worship and their theological basis. Martineau was a complicated thinker and theologian who wrestled continually with questions concerning the sources of authority, the position of Christ in Christianity, the validity of non-Christian religions, the roles of reason and conscience, the Bible, and his own tenuous relationship with the Unitarian denomination. He left no written account of his theory of worship, but his ideas can be inferred from numerous references in sermons and lectures at the College, where he taught for 45 years, and where he was principal for 16 years. His ideas can be deduced further from his hymnals, his prayer book, and the memoirs of friends who described his thinking and ministry.

Among other topics, this book will examine Martineau's ideas about sermons, prayer, ritual, his vision of human nature, and his understanding of the impact on religion of the many explorations, discoveries, and scientific developments of his time. Other chapters in this book examine his struggle with the question of authority and outline his theology.

So few of the orders of service Martineau used in his churches have been preserved that it is impossible to tell how their form evolved except from his own scattered references. This book, therefore, will focus primarily on his mature ideas as reflected in his last major works. Martineau's beliefs changed through his many years of reflection and practice, and those changes are noted where appropriate. He made no apologies for the changes in his thought. It was characteristic of him to say, "It would be a strange result of a studious man's reading and reflection, did he find that he had nothing to learn and nothing to unlearn, but could still believe at fifty precisely what he set down at twenty five."[2] For example, Martineau's 1862 prayer book had a great influence on Unitarianism, yet earlier in his career he had scorned the very idea of prayer books. There are also significant differences between the hymnals he edited throughout his career, and his use of the Bible as an authority changed with developments in biblical criticism.

The intent of the book is to examine Martineau's theory of worship in the context of his theology, and its influence on Unitarian thought. This book will begin with a brief biographical sketch and a discussion of the main influences on Martineau's thought (Chapter I). It proceeds to examine Martineau's ideas on the theory and the practice of worship (Chapter II), and on how the minister, as a leader of public worship, must carry out Martineau's ideas as a servant of God (Chapter III). It also traces Martineau's long struggle with the question of authority, moving from reliance on the Bible and Christian tradition to reason as the most direct means of access to divine knowledge, and finally to the moral law and conscience (Chapter IV). Martineau pondered the question of the source of the minister's authority in worship: from God, as Martineau believed, or by the congregation, the denomination, or the state? Finally, the book outlines Martineau's theology and indicates how his ideas on worship derive from his beliefs (Chapter V).

As we will see, Martineau brought new insight and self-confidence to a dispirited religious group. His influence continues: his hymns are still sung, his prayers are still used, and his writings still instruct people. His contribution to hymnody and liturgy, through his books of prayers, hymns, and his collection *Common Prayer for Christian Worship*, charted a new course for Unitarian churches. The contention of this book, however, is that Martineau's greatest contribution lay in strengthening the theological basis for worship and giving a strong liturgical impulse to the Unitarian churches.

While Martineau's career has been explored by other scholars, none has focused on his understanding of worship. Previous work on Martineau consists of a fine biography by Joseph Estlin Carpenter, *James Martineau* (1905), and James Drummond and C. B. Upton's two-volume *Life and Letters of James Martineau* (1905), both of which tangentially address his views on worship. Several articles and memorials immediately after his death briefly discuss his role as a preacher. Ralph Waller's Ph.D. dissertation (1986) has an important section dealing with Martineau's ecclesiology, and other authors, such as Horton Davies (1962), have offered brief evaluations of Martineau's liturgical ability. There are, however, no books, dissertations, or articles that deal with his views on worship directly at any length.

Notes

1. Schneewind, 237. Only short citations are given in the notes; please see the Bibliography for full details.
2. Studies, vi.

Chapter I: Biography and Influences

1. Martineau's Life

James Martineau (1805–1900) was the youngest of the seven children of Thomas (d. 1826) and Elizabeth (d. 1848) Martineau, who were of Huguenot stock. His father was a cloth manufacturer and wine merchant. At the time of his birth, Martineau's parents were members of the Octagon Chapel in Norwich. The Chapel was Presbyterian but inclined toward Unitarianism and officially became Unitarian in 1813, when Martineau was eight.[1] In 1828, Martineau married Helen Higginson (1802–1876), daughter of the Rev. Edward Higginson, a Unitarian minister in Derby. The couple had eight children, including a daughter who died in infancy.

In 1822 Martineau entered Manchester College in York, one of the leading Dissenting Academies, then under the principalship of Charles Wellbeloved. Martineau was a man of impressive stature and demeanor. He was adored by those who knew him, and spoken well of by his peers. Charles Wicksteed, a leading British intellectual and a Unitarian minister, as well as a close friend of Martineau, described Martineau thus:

> Well does the writer remember, though it is forty-five years ago, how the circular staircase of the somewhat conspicuous pulpit [Paradise Street Chapel, Liverpool] was quietly ascended by a tall young man, thin, but of vigorous and muscular frame, with dark hair, pale but not delicate complexion, a countenance full in repose of thought, and in animation of intelligence and enthusiasm, features belonging to no regular type or order of beauty, and yet leaving the impression of a very high kind of

beauty, and a voice so sweet, and clear, and strong, without being in the least degree loud, that it conveyed all the inspiration of music without any of its art or intention.²

Henry Gow, a student at Manchester College from 1879 to 1884, described Martineau in similar terms: "I remember his rich, deep, gentle voice: his wonderful humility, his exquisite graciousness and eager sympathy."³

During his career, Martineau held three pastorates. His first was at Eustace Street Chapel, Dublin, from 1828 to 1831. He resigned in protest over the regium donum;⁴ the resignation was accepted by a majority of one. His second church was Paradise Street Chapel, Liverpool, where he went in 1832 as colleague to John Grundy; in 1835 he became sole pastor. In 1849 the Chapel moved to, and changed its name to, Hope Street. He resigned in 1857 after a ministry of 25 years. His third charge was a co-ministry with John James Tayler at Little Portland Street Chapel, London, from 1859 to 1872, while he was a professor at Manchester College.

In 1840 Martineau became Professor of Mental and Moral Philosophy and Political Economy at Manchester New College, then located in Manchester. In 1853 Manchester College moved to London, and for four years Martineau commuted from Liverpool to deliver his lectures. In 1857 he resigned his ministry in Liverpool and moved to London. He continued lecturing there until 1885, when he was 80, and served as principal from 1869 to 1885. He was then elected to the honorary position of President of the College.

Martineau's activities beyond his churches and the college were few, but they did include writing for the *London Review* and the *Theological Review* and editing the *Prospective Review* and its successor, *National Review*. He helped form the Free Christian Union, and he was a member of the Metaphysical Society, founded by Lord Tennyson, with whom he developed a close friendship. He held a prestigious and influential position as trustee of Dr. [Daniel] Williams's Trust, which had been established in the 18th century for the further education of the clergy.

Martineau was a gentle man, but his life was not free from controversy. His *Rationale of Religious Enquiry* (1836), which exalted reason above Scripture as an authority, marked him as a dangerous radical among the older Unitarians. In 1839, in an episode known as "the Liverpool Controversy," Martineau and two colleagues, John Hamilton Thom and Henry Giles, engaged in public disputation with members of the Anglican clergy, led by Fielding Ould, the vicar of Christ Church, Liverpool, over the Trinitarian-Unitarian interpretation of Scripture. Later, in March 1851, Martineau broke permanently with his sister, Harriet, over his review "Mesmeric Atheism," published in *Prospective Review*, of Henry George Atkinson's *Letters on the Laws of Man's Nature and Development*, which Harriet had edited. Apparently the split occurred because Harriet had adopted the philosophy of positivism, of which James disapproved.

A further controversy occurred in 1866, when the Chair of the Philosophy of Mind and Logic became vacant at University College and Martineau applied for the position. He was considered to have outstanding qualifications but was rejected.[5] In protest, one university professor resigned his chair, and the Council of University College was subjected to severe criticism by many of the faculty and others who saw its move as a betrayal of their trust.

Controversy, however, did not prevent Martineau's influence from spreading. In time Martineau's contributions to scholarship were recognized in countries and universities on both sides of the Atlantic. Martineau received honorary degrees from five universities in as many countries: an LL.D. from Harvard in 1872; an S.Th.D. from Leyden in 1875; a D.D. from Edinburgh in 1884; a D.C.L. *honoris causa* from Oxford in 1888; and a Litt.D. from Dublin in 1892. Martineau's books were published widely in the United States, and many of his sermons were translated into German and Dutch.

2. Martineau's Character

Martineau said modestly of himself, "As to what I have done in a long career, it has been the simplest thing in the world. It has been simply to say precisely and always that which I thought and believed and felt to be true: to hold back nothing, to profess nothing and to measure nothing by a standard other than was perfectly and absolutely sincere."[6] Martineau was a scholarly man whose adventures of the mind strengthened the intellectual life of England. He was devoted to his friends, though he did not make friends easily. He was at home with serious conversation, uncomfortable with small talk and offended by any flippancy or vulgarity, although he often won over people more serious than himself. He was a highly disciplined man. He held strong convictions, which he would rethink when occasion warranted. He held typical Victorian views about the need to develop strength of character. Martineau never smoked, and he gave up drinking at several points in his life. An excellent businessman and an avid correspondent, he had a refined and gentle demeanor, with a dignified modesty and courtly grace in his conversation. His sermon delivery was vivid and dramatic, unlike his relatively mechanical delivery of lectures, but he did not gesticulate or make much use of "body language." The sermons were always serious, without any touch of humor or irony. Martineau's politics were of the old Whig school, and he aroused some dislike by siding with the South in the American Civil War because of his conviction that the North was wrong in using force to settle a moral question. He also opposed home rule for Ireland because of his belief that the nation must be kept intact, and providing home rule for Ireland would raise the same divisive issue for Scotland and Wales. The 1901 edition of *The Dictionary of National Biography* adds that he was opposed to free education.[7] Like many other Victorians, he believed people should make their own way without dependence on charity or largesse from the state.

Religiously, Martineau was a pietist in the sense that he believed religion must concern itself with individual regeneration rather than social movements. Social justice, he thought, should be a consequence of theology, not a replacement for it. He said he wanted a "Christianity purified of superstitions, a Church intent only on Righteousness, and a Social habit of justice and charity to all men."[8] His sermons advocated no political or social causes and were concerned only with the soul. From the Pietists, Martineau also adopted a belief in the importance of the individual as opposed to organizations, in the kind of sturdy self-reliance that guided Emerson's thinking as well.

Never in his life did Martineau compromise his integrity, and people who knew him best considered that his most impressive trait. Alexander Craufurd, an Anglican priest who knew him well, writes:

> Of all his qualities I think the one which impressed me most at first in this Unitarian philosopher was his absolute integrity, his great though entirely unobtrusive sanctity. . . . It seemed to be almost impossible that this saint of Theism had ever done anything morally wrong. . . . Flippancy always jarred on him painfully. . . . Of purely intellectual differences my teacher was extremely tolerant. . . .[9]

However, Craufurd also tells us that Martineau was not the solemn, Puritanical type people would suppose if they knew him mainly from his sermons. Martineau also enjoyed humor, liked to hear amusing stories, and enjoyed genial company.[10]

By the end of his life, Martineau was recognized as a great religious thinker. On his 83rd birthday he received a letter signed by Lord Tennyson, Robert Browning, Benjamin Jowett, Ernst Renan, William James, Joseph Chamberlain, James Russell Lowell, Charles Eliot, and many others from both sides of the Atlantic. It read, in part, "We desire to express to you, on your eighty-third birthday, the feelings of reverence and affection which are entertained towards you, not only by your own Communion, but by members of other Christian Churches who are acquainted with your character and writings." Yet, though others regarded his accomplishments so highly, Martineau considered that he simply had followed duty and obeyed the demands of conscience. To the accolade of those great ones, Martineau replied with characteristic modesty, "To be held of any account by the elite of those to whom I have habitually looked up, including representatives from the foremost ranks of literature, science, philosophy, religion, and person[al] character, is an honour simply mysterious to me."[11] Though others considered him a great man, Martineau himself did not see himself in that light.

Although Martineau's theology was Unitarian, he did not wish to be bound by denominational labels:

> I have always made it a point of conscience to ask when I am invited either to subscribe to or to open a new chapel—"What is the paramount principle of your association? What is your trust deed? Is it open or is it closed? Is it for Christian worship, or is it, on the other hand, simply for Unitarian worship?" It has always been a point of conscience with me to refrain, either from aiding by money, or from opening, by personal service, chapels dedicated simply to Unitarian, or Trinitarian, or any doctrinal cause.[12]

3. Influences

Martineau was strongly influenced in his ministry by Charles Wellbeloved (1769–1858), the principal of Manchester College in York while Martineau was a student there. He also acknowledged a debt to Ralph Waldo Emerson. He admired and was influenced by the American theologian William Ellery Channing (1780–1842), an older contemporary and, in some respects, his American counterpart. Channing in turn admired Martineau's thinking. Channing was the intellectual leader of American Unitarianism and opposed Calvinism in America much as Martineau opposed Anglicanism in England. Both were Unitarian in theology but indifferent toward Unitarianism as an organized movement, and for the same reason: they both believed the organization impeded the growth of the spirit by stressing doctrinal grounds for union. Martineau was impressed by David Friedrich Strauss' *Life of Jesus* (1835) and Theodore Parker's *Discourse of Matters Pertaining to Religion* (1842), but he thought more highly of the historical basis of the Gospels than did Strauss.

While Paradise Street Chapel in Liverpool was being rebuilt in 1847, Martineau left for 15 months in Germany. Much of his time in Berlin was spent reading under Adolph Trendelenburg (1802–1872), a professor at the University of Berlin, prolific writer, and philologist. Today, Trendelenburg is remembered for his criticisms of Kant and Hegel based on the thought of Plato and Aristotle. While in Germany, Martineau studied Plato and Kant, both of whom influenced his thinking strongly. Plato's philosophy was the basis for Martineau's own idealist philosophy.

Martineau's religion derived much from Kant, especially Kant's emphasis on God, freedom, duty, and immortality, and he expressed his reliance on Kant at the end of his work *Types of Ethical Theory* (1885):

> It is scarcely less a surprise to myself than it can be to my readers, that no pages of this book have been reserved for Kant. The reason, paradoxical as it may seem, is found not in any slight of his ethical theory, but in an approximate adoption of it; so that if, in working at my subjects, my thoughts seldom consciously encountered his, it was from coalescence too near for adequate difference.[13]

Ralph Waller notes that Martineau's *The Study of Religion* (1888) contains 60 references to Kant, including some elaborate treatments of Kant's major ideas on free will, duty, and belief in immortality.[14]

As Horton Davies notes, however, "the Pietism which was in Kant's background displays itself in the foreground of Martineau's concern.... Martineau had the sensitivity of the artist and the poet, and his religion ... is marked by a profound sense of dependence upon God, and of the importance of experience in renewing man's relationship to God and his fellows."[15] Kant provided the developed form of idealist philosophy which combined with Martineau's theology so well. Martineau also learned from Kant's ideas on duty and freedom as a condition of moral obligation: "[I]f I have a duty then this must be something I am capable of fulfilling, the 'ought' implies 'I can.'"[16]

While in Germany, Martineau studied and rejected Hegel because he found him exceptionally difficult and obscure. The effect of his study, he said, was to throw him back to the position of Kant on Idealism.[17] According to his biographer Carpenter, Martineau always retained that disdain for Hegel: "And when English philosophy at length opened itself to the witcheries of the Hegelian idealism he could see no fresh truth in the system which he had studied, and rejected, a generation before."[18] Martineau's response to Schleiermacher, on the other hand—from whom he derived much of his own thinking about Idealism and conscience—

was qualified approval. Schleiermacher persuaded thoughtful people to renew their interest in religion, but Martineau saw a flaw: a consciousness of dependence on God would cause people to become too introspective, to subordinate the objective reality of God as a source of knowledge to their own subjective perceptions.

Martineau was also strongly influenced by the idealist position that the mind is immortal and indestructible. The mind, he said, is that which provides us with divine aspirations in the form of the conscience, which is "an internal Deity known to immediate consciousness. . . . [I]t was thus that he [God] was discerned by Jesus, and so revealed to us."[19] The physical universe, he said, is the manifestation and abode of God, as indeed we are. The universe is "the autobiography of the Infinite Spirit, repeating itself in miniature within our Finite Spirit."[20] The universe is a mirror of God's thought. We must see the universe not only as intelligible but also as a product of Intelligence. Nature, said Martineau, provides insights about God; we look into nature and find objects that give us an apprehension of God. Martineau warned that we err if we look at nature and see nothing beyond: "God has not bound himself all up in the routine of nature, that we should seek him there alone, where is only the material fabric of his hand, and not the spiritual likeness of himself."[21] Martineau was also attracted to the union in idealist philosophy of the intellect with devoutness. He said the philosophy of idealism becomes religion when we affirm that we are subservient and related to an All-perfect Mind: "Devout faith is a belief of real Being on the strength of what ought to be."[22]

Although idealism did not give way to positivism until the twentieth century,[23] the positivist trend was already present in Martineau's day. Martineau witnessed the growing influence of its founder Comte and feared its potential impact on religious faith. Martineau wrote of the weakening effects of science, invention, exploration, and technology on the religious spirit. Such modern developments, he said, distracted the spirit and caused people to turn their attention to trifles and gadgets, to look to cause and effect for explanations of the creative and renewing spirit. He wrote: "We must contradict the doctrine of mere science, which proclaims Force, rather than Thought, as the source of it all. . . . If it takes mind to construe the world, how can the negation of mind suffice to constitute it?"[24] The growth of positivism sharpened Martineau's conviction that the spirit must be dominant over passion, and determined him to rely more heavily on the indwelling God.

Notes

1. In the England of Martineau's day, there were three primary dissenting bodies. The General Baptists were similar to the American Universalists in that they believed in adult baptism and believed that everyone would be saved. Eventually the General Baptists, always a small group, became Unitarian. Another group was the Independents, who later called themselves Congregationalists. Finally, the Presbyterians believed in the sufficiency of the Bible. They rejected creeds and formulations because they were non-biblical. They referred to themselves as "English Presbyterians" to distinguish themselves from the rigid Scottish Presbyterians. However, no churches bore the name "English Presbyterian." Over time, the English Presbyterians became more liberal, and most of them became Unitarian.
2. *In Memoriam James Martineau 1805–1900*, 7. In 1832, at the time of the memory he recalls here, Wicksteed was Minister of the Ancient Chapel of Toxteth.
3. *Ibid.*, 29.
4. The *regium donum* was an annual allowance to Presbyterian ministers from the Crown that had been made since 1690. It became Martineau's grant when Philip Taylor, his senior colleague, died. Martineau refused it because he believed it would be an injustice to take money from the government that was denied to priests in the Catholic Church. The amount in question was 100 pounds sterling per year.
5. According to *In Memoriam James Martineau 1805–1900*, he was rejected "on the ground that he was a Unitarian minister, and was not therefore to be trusted as an impartial student of philosophy" (15). However, that appears to be incorrect. Martineau's rejection was due to his being a minister, not specifically because he was a Unitarian minister.
6. "The Church of the Future, a speech Delivered by the Rev. James Martineau, at the Hope-Street School-Rooms, Liverpool, on Monday, September 25, 1871," 4.
7. *Dictionary of National Biography*, Supplemental Vol. III (1901), 150.
8. "Presentation to The Reverend James Martineau, June 1872," 13.
9. Craufurd, 8–9.
10. *Ibid.*, 12.
11. "Address, Presented to James Martineau, D.D., LL.D., On his Eighty-third Birthday, April 21, 1888, and Dr. Martineau's Reply; with A List of Signatures," 22.
12. "The Church of the Future," 6.
13. *Types of Ethical Theory* II, 522.

14. Waller, James Martineau, 523.
15. Horton Davies, 268.
16. Lewis, 280.
17. Drummond and Upton I, 330.
18. Carpenter, 550.
19. *National Duties*, 234.
20. "Nature and God," 14.
21. *Ibid.*, 10.
22. *Essays IV*, 277.
23. Lewis (1985), 273.
24. *Essays IV*, 461, 173.

Chapter II: Martineau's Theory of Worship

1. Overview

Curiously, Martineau never wrote or preached on worship, although he spent his life as a minister and taught ministers. His thoughts on worship must be inferred from references in his sermons, prayers, hymnals, and his *Common Prayer for Christian Worship*. We will examine his general theory of the nature and purpose of worship. He wrestled with the tension between the free spirit and regularized worship. After all, Martineau helped spread the term "Free Christian Church" instead of using a denominational label, and yet he wrote and advocated a prayer book, though he urged caution in its use. We will examine Martineau's ideas on rites, particularly baptism and the Lord's Supper. We need to see how the various elements of worship, especially prayers and hymns, accorded with his theory. Finally, we will look at Martineau's views on how sermons ought to be used in worship.

Martineau was an author, lecturer, educator, philosopher, theologian, and minister, yet he considered his most important task that of conducting public worship. Accordingly, he paid great attention to his own demeanor in leading worship. His early biographer A. W. Jackson describes his worship manner thus:

> A tall, spare figure robed in the scholar's gown, and wearing the dignities of his office as a natural grace; a thin face, suggestive of the cloister, and traced with deep lines of thought; a voice not loud, but musical and reaching; an enunciation leisurely but not slow, and perfectly distinct. The opening services are some-

what long, but informed by a spirit that lifts them above tedium. The hymn is read in tones that reveal a soul that vibrates to its melody and thrills to its joy. There is reverent reading of the Scriptures, reading not obtrusive as to its emphasis, but which reveals their meaning and conveys their power. The prayer is quiet, tender, appealing, a strain of rapture and love and longing.[1]

Worship was of paramount importance to Martineau, the minister's way of awakening people to an awareness of their true nature and divine potential. Martineau saw a need to strengthen the Unitarian worship practices of his day. John Stoughton, the Congregationalist historian, characterized Unitarian worship as the reason for the movement's decline in numbers and power. Although oversimplified, his observations are important:

> A dry, hard, cold method of preaching generally marked the pulpit; warm, vigorous spiritual life, appeared not in the pews. No greater contrast can be imagined, than between the Methodist and the Presbyterian [i.e., Unitarian] preacher, the Methodists and the Presbyterian people. The unction, the fire, the moral force so visible in the one case, is absent in the other. Methodism laid hold on the conscience of England; Presbyterianism did not.[2]

According to Martineau, worship had several characteristics. First, he said, worship is an expression of the soul that combines reason with a sense of the awesome majesty of God's presence. Martineau saw it as a drama of the great mystery in which God's care for people was experienced. Liturgy, he said, lends stability to a confused and precarious existence. The aim of worship is not to feel good or make friends; it is to draw the person closer to God. People approach God through purity of heart. The minister's role is to declare the truth and to remind people of the divine promise: "It is my office and my joy, to be the mere organ and vehicle of truths and sanctities, that claim and command us all."[3]

In worship, said Martineau, people aim to conform to the holy, to become conscious of their connection with the divine. Worship should be "the image and shadow of Heavenly things" and remind people of their true nature: "Whoever truly worships, pouring out the prayer, not of interest and fear, nor chiefly of personal gratitude, but of aspiration, reverence and trust, feels irresistibly assured that he is yielding to no weakness, but is falling into the attitude congenial to higher natures."[4] In worship, Martineau believed, the spirit reaches out to unite with God:

> We come to worship with confidence in our own powers to approach God. We begin not with a sense of human depravity or terror before God, nor with that distrust in our own powers that causes us to want mediators, but with a conviction that our piety and devotion will bring us closer to an understanding of God and righteousness. We come to church, by a common quest of some holy spirit to penetrate and purify our life; by a common desire to quit its hot and level dust, and from its upland slopes of contemplation inhale the serenity of God . . . and give us a more intimate view, of that fathomless eternity, wherein so many dear and mortal things have dropped from our imploring eyes.[5]

Martineau opposed what he saw as trends destructive of the spirit, such as the utilitarian view that worship ought to have some usefulness beyond opening the soul to divine inspiration. In *Hymns for the Christian Church*,[6] he said people should be wary of any ulterior purpose, even instruction, exposition, or persuasion. "Worship is not for a purpose, but from an emotion."[7] We should not judge worship by its consequences but by its ability to unite us with God. Worship is an end, not a means:

> Those who ask, or who would explain, what is it for . . . have as absolutely lost its true spirit, as the mother would forget her nature, if she were to regulate her caresses by expediency. The plaints of a sacred sorrow, the cry of penitence, the vow of duty, the brilliancy of praise, shed forth, like the laughter and the tears of infancy, from a heart conscious of nothing else, are examples of the true and primitive devotion.[8]

Although he felt emotion played a significant role in worship, Martineau was also a rationalist. He believed faith was primarily emotional, but he also wanted worship to be based on an intelligent understanding. However, he also knew that rationalist devotion, in its concern for understanding, often lacked the spirit of poetry. Religion, he said, must use symbolic language because the great truths it holds are beyond literal language. For Martineau, reason is a guide to truth but by itself is not sufficient for the understanding. We need to think conceptually and go beyond reason, but without contradicting it. Thus parable and poetry are necessary for the spirit to approach God. Worship uses metaphor, not literal speech. Martineau speaks of "a petty rationalism that . . . wanders altogether from the spirit of truth. At best when we try to speak to God, religion sinks with the utterance, and seems to become poor."[9]

Early in his career, Martineau relied on reason as the final arbiter of belief. As he aged, however, he came to believe there are higher sources of authority, especially intuition and conscience. He grew to believe it was inadequate in guiding the spirit. Although he said belief must not contradict reason, and reason is an arbiter in doctrine, his awareness of the spiritual threats from increasing reliance on science and technology led him to be wary of an excessive reliance on reason. Worship, said Martineau, relies more on the spirit than on reason. It must promote enthusiasm, aspiration, and impulsive escape into communion with the divine. Religion errs, said Martineau, when it focuses too narrowly on moral strictures: "It was not to keep men temperate and honest that the vaulted Minster was raised, or the Sanctus pealed through its aisles."[10] That is, reason is not sufficient for the devotional life; we must also rely on the influx of God.

In addition, Martineau wanted worship to remove the distractions of a culture that turned people toward what he saw as "worship of Strength."[11] "It has become fashionable," he said, "to admire, in commerce, gigantic operations; in politics, visible success; in literature, negligent force & vivid colouring."[12] He saw people turn away from worship because it seemed to them outmoded. He sensed that the newspaper would replace the preacher and prophet, that science would replace the zeal for moral inspiration, and that "this sphere of being will then be perfectly administered when no reference to another distracts attention."[13]

He also saw the need to recover vitality in worship as a counter to rote worship, a habit that can become so like an instinct that spiritually one becomes like a person asleep.[14]

Martineau also spoke against any form of sectarianism. "We profess to have no Christ exclusively our own," he said in dedicating a church.[15] Sectarianism is a negative force centering on belief and creed: "Let no presuming creed, let no cold formalism enter here; but let the objects which should be loved, for ever transcend the notions that should be thought."[16] Sectarianism, he said, deters the free search for God. Martineau believed there should be unity of purpose and agreement in broad terms on questions of belief within an individual church, but that churches need not agree with each other. A denomination, he said, should provide services such as printing hymnals and worship material and supervising the training of ministers, but should not establish rules and regulations that interfere with local church prerogatives.

Martineau's ideas on worship incorporated his (and Kant's) broader philosophy of freedom, duty, and immortality. He struggled to unite his belief in reason with the search for faith. With his strong sense of dependence on God, he approached worship with the sensitivity of an artist or poet. Davies suggests that Martineau was influenced by Presbyterian ideas on the majesty of God and the duty of humankind to glorify Him, though Martineau rejected the ideas of original sin, predestination, and election. He also rejected the Anglican idea of "a common formulary of prayer, with a chaste and carefully chosen diction, balanced cadences, and responses," designed to make worship truly corporate.[17] Public worship, he believed, must not follow procedures that limit access to God to narrow channels. Thus Davies calls Martineau "a Pietist in the Rationalist tradition."[18]

2. The Nature and Purpose of Worship

According to Martineau, worship was the central purpose of the church. It took precedence over all other functions, even that of instruction, though Martineau as an educator and philosopher had high regard for that role as well. Worship explores our relationship and duty to God, and Martineau believed worship would have less value without the concept of a personal God—by which Martineau meant not a God with personal human characteristics, but a God with whom we have a personal relation: "I cannot conceive of a Church without worship of a Living and Personal God. With this, I think, a Church must begin, not end: and short of this we can have,—as it seems to me,—only clubs or associations for particular objects, not any fusion into a common spiritual life."[19] In Martineau's vision, the church is a worshiping community, and worship seeks to reunite us with God: "It is [the soul's] effort to return home."[20] We surrender our self-will in order to merge with the divine. In worship at its best, we sense that we mingle with God.

In worship, said Martineau, the soul reaches to God as we offer ourselves to fulfill our sacred mission as divine beings. We aim at holiness, and if our worship is earnest we gain an insight into that perfection which brings us a touch of grace. Worship, he said, is the free offering of ourselves to God, but it is ever imperfect. The soul seeks its home by surrender of the self-will, and prayer directs us toward merger with the divine. We live, said Martineau, amid turmoil, tragedy, and distractions. We are tempted to turn aside from the pressing demands of the spirit and escape from guilt and responsibility to a life of minimal searching, in the process neglecting worship. Yet in so doing we starve the soul.

Through worship, Martineau attempted to nurture the divine spirit within, to open the soul to the love of God, and in consequence to help us understand our duties toward God. Martineau believed people should seek to cultivate personal devotion to God during worship, not to expand their intellectual understanding of theology:

> It [the church] is not dedicated to your convictions or to my convictions: it is dedicated to worship and service of the ever-living and true God, and those who enter it should do so, not for a theological object, but for a religious and devout object—to prostrate their souls before the maker and the ruler of us all, to train their consciences for the duty of life, to find consolation for the trials, troubles, and sorrows of life, and to look forward with unfeigned aspiration towards the greater future that

> awaits us all. . . . [T]he liberty of the soul should not be restrained. . . . [T]he soul shall be free to take its flight whithersoever the inspiration of the spirit of God shall carry it.[21]

Like intellectual discussions, theological creeds had no place in Martineau's conception of worship. Martineau shunned creeds because he believed they restricted religion, which must remain free to grow in understanding and open to new inspiration. This freedom is central to the tradition of English Presbyterianism, to which Martineau felt close. One of his objections to the Anglican *Book of Common Prayer* was that, though it achieved great eloquence and beauty in its language, it forestalled the search for further truth. He followed the Puritan idea that devotion should be a free outpouring of the spirit, and that God has more truth and light yet to break forth out of his holy word.

In contrast to the formulas of intellect and creed, for Martineau, worship can best be understood through an artistic model. The sentiments of worship, he said, have inspired architecture, music, painting, and poetry. These disciplines were originally expressions of the sacred, and if we retain a sense of art and aesthetics we are more likely to enter into the spirit of holiness. Thus can inspiration open our vision to a better self. We need to focus on something greater and beyond, something invisible. And we must approach worship with the confidence that God is also real, even if God cannot be perceived in the universe with the senses:

> It is inconceivable . . . that what is most real and commanding with us should come of stretching the soul into the unreal and empty. . . . I am persuaded, that life would soon become intolerable on earth, were it copied from nothing in the heavens; that its deeper affections would pine away and its lights of purest thought grow pale, if it lay shrouded in no Holy Spirit, but only in the wilderness of space. . . . Never can the world be less to us, than when we make it focus all in all.[22]

Though he did not believe in the Calvinist doctrine of human depravity, Martineau did speak of the need to recognize sin as we strive to encourage our native goodness. Worship must help us overcome our proclivity to sin and evil in its many forms. Worship achieves its highest value in helping us to strengthen the instincts planted in us by conscience, which prods us to seek union with God. Our striving for that union is evidence of our divine nature, "for like only can commune with like.... Devotion instinctively tries to lay down whatever separates us from God, and to pass wholly into what unites with him. It takes its stand on the felt common ground, the points of meeting, between the human and the Divine."[23] In addition to promoting union with God, said Martineau, worship aims at inspiring reverence and prepares us to receive revelation. Further, we do not need a special revelation; revelation is always available.

Martineau also stressed the need to worship in community rather than alone. Worship can be solitary, but a mystical level of communion develops when people gather for worship, when hearts and voices join in prayers and hymns. The truth becomes clearer when people thus support each other.

Worship, said Martineau, strengthens our relation with God. Here, he agreed with Ninian Smart, who has written: "God is reached down a certain corridor, according to my analysis, and this is the corridor of worship."[24] Worship requires an object, and the object is God. Worship then is a turning to God, which is as natural as the infant's eye turning to the light.[25] Worship must be more than just a a search for moral certainty, or a wish to become a better person. Morality is not a substitute for worship, but a consequence of it. Consciousness of sin and failure, the experience of grief and want, prick the conscience and influence the individual to seek communion with God. Thus, worship is far more than the effort to make people honest and virtuous. Worship attempts to join the human spirit with the Divine. It is both an escape from the world of false values and distractions and a confrontation of it. Worship prepares us for a higher communion, similar to that of Jesus, and it should, "resemble his who, in fullness of the Spirit, 'went, as his custom was, into the synagogue on the Sabbath day,' [to] prepare for a higher communion, where 'your life is hid with him in God.'"[26]

We expect the church to direct our reverence and cleanse the spirit of the intrusions that deter us from true worship, Martineau said. In the church we should find a Christian conception of what is noble and beautiful. And it is reverence that makes us most truly human. Without worship we are something less than human. Martineau believed that human society originated in people's joining to seek divine guidance. Primitive people would have found no other purpose so strong as appealing to the holy, which may have stemmed from wonder. Primitive forms of worship, said Martineau, provided a bond that found expression in a variety of ways, such as art, caste, sacred literature, and, indeed, the very origins of civilization. For Martineau, veneration is so distinctive a human trait that it defines what we mean by "human."

The emotions of worship, said Martineau, must be transformed from guilt and terror into love, trust, and aspiration. Worship must turn away from sin and shame and any tendencies that impede our access to the divine.[27] Worship is innate within us because of the divine within us, and Martineau stressed the direct relation of the soul to God. Martineau understood the human conscience to be not the voice of God speaking to us, but the voice of God speaking within us: "the Kingdom of God is within you." Thus the impulse to seek the holy is natural: "It does not depend on special knowledge, on natural abilities which are distributed unequally by a stepmotherly nature, on worldly wealth or position. It depends only on our trying as hard as we can to live as we ought—to pattern ourselves after the perfect exemplar whom God has sent us as a guide."[28] Martineau saw this life as a probationary period: we are in God's hands, and what God looks for in us is not our accomplishments, but our efforts.

For Martineau, worship was not to be trivial or multi-focused. We only dilute worship, he said, by using the distractions of clever quotations, anecdotes, or—a quality anathema to Martineau—humor. When Manchester College moved from London to Oxford and opened its new facilities, Martineau said in a communion address, "Brethren in the Fellowship of Christ,—We have dedicated this building to the service of God in spirit and in truth. It remains that we dedicate ourselves, in all our use of it and the life within it, to the highest claims of the Spirit and the surest leadings of the Truth."[29]

Martineau had a clear and exact concept of the content of worship. In his *Biographical Memoranda* he wrote, "The hours set apart for public worship should be absolutely surrendered, as it seems to me, to devout thought and utterance and the consecration of human life by Divine affections; and as a rule I could never, without feeling myself guilty of an abuse, treat the pulpit as a lecturer's platform, for didactic exposition, critical discussion, or philosophical speculation."[30] Martineau recognized the need for administrative routine, the teaching function, and study of Scripture at times other than during worship, but he said, "I limited the sermon, as far as possible, to the positive elements of spiritual faith, and reserved for the lecture-room the apparatus and process of proof and refutation."[31] Similarly, when the new Hope Street Church was opened in Liverpool, he said:

> We dedicate our church to no creed. . . . [W]e raise here, not a school, but a church; not a hall of debate, but a shrine of God; and shall collect, not a parliament of critics, but a brotherhood of worshippers. For this end there must be a faith in each not wandering very far from the faith of all. Only where there is essentially one heart and mind can the many find themselves represented by the breathings of a single spirit.[32]

3. Martineau's Prayer Book

Martineau questioned whether worship should be regularized. A fixed liturgy deters the free spirit, he believed, yet he also acknowledged that prayer books were valued by major portions of Christianity. At the beginning of his career, Martineau disliked prayer books, both in theory and in practice. He said with scorn, "Prayer by the printing-press is surely a very near approach to piety by machinery."[33] He reasoned that prayer ought to be a struggle within the worshipper's spirit. Worship should be a confrontation and an opening of the soul to receive such inspiration as may come freely. He objected to prayer books because worship can easily become rote. With a prayer book in hand, worship becomes a matter of "saying our prayers."[34] The words to be recited are on a printed page, and habit becomes so strong that one finds it difficult to pray without that guide. With a prayer book in hand—Anglican or Unitarian—Martineau feared that "the words have little real meaning for those who utter them;

and that precisely the minds of deepest sincerity and most susceptible piety are the least at home in them."[35]

Through reflection and efforts to achieve a worship that is meaningful and beautiful but which does not restrict the free search, however, Martineau gradually came to see the value of prayer books in enhancing worship. He saw much to criticize in the worship of his day. He disliked the two opposing trends within the Dissenting tradition of Evangelism and Rationalism, both of which, he wrote, "have carried the ugliness of Protestantism to the fullest extent."[36] Rationalism, thought Martineau, tends toward coldness and is limited by confining itself to logic and sensory perception. Yet Evangelism is too impulsive and can be thoughtless. Martineau wanted a worship that could retain the free spirit of Dissent and the dignity of the Established Church.

Martineau believed that many of his fellow ministers were too anxious to express theological and philosophical ideas at the expense of inspiring worship. The typical Unitarian worship of Martineau's time consisted of an alternation of hymns, prayers, and readings surrounding the sermon, which was often considered the most important aspect of the service, to the neglect of the liturgy. Even stately occasions followed that usual form. For example, at the induction of the Rev. Alexander Gordon as minister of Hope Street Church in Liverpool, where Martineau had served before him, worship consisted of a hymn, prayer, lesson, hymn, charge (by Martineau), organ voluntary, Right Hand of Fellowship, Acceptance by the minister, hymn, then Collection and Benediction. Such a liturgy need not be elaborate, said Martineau, but it should have a sense of continuity—which a prayer book could help to provide.

Martineau had a strong poetic as well as rationalist temperament, and he felt the need for a better-developed liturgical strain in the Unitarian churches. Worship, said Martineau, must move below the superficial to plumb the depths and meanings of life: "All the pathetic appeals and reverent usages of life," he said, "the patient love, the costly pity, lavished on sorrow and infirmity, all the graceful ceremonial of the affections at the birth, the marriage, and the funeral, assume that everywhere more is than seems; that whatever happens has holier meanings than we can tell. . . ."[37]

A good liturgy, one that uses lofty language and symbolism, need not restrain the spirit but can act as a guide to give meaning to both the ordinary and the special parts of life. Martineau noted that it is symbolism that converts a house to a home, food into a meal, or a pit into a grave. Ritual, he said, can lift us above the literal and provide an interpretation of life based on love, awe, and admiration; it can be an aid to our sense of duty and justice. Martineau had inherited the stark Puritan tradition, but he wrote of the need to soften it and reintroduce the arts, to allow the senses to act upon the soul.[38] Worship that becomes rote loses its claim to moral persuasion: "When the regularities of habit and the perseverance of all become simply automatic, they lose their claim to moral admiration: however they may pace with heavier grist the mill of wealth, they have ever less to offer at the shrine of worship: the windows are darkened through which gleams of divine and solemn light once entered and enriched the soul. . . ."[39]

Martineau recognized that individualism must somehow be reconciled to corporate worship and devotion. A devout life should also be a regulated life, he said: "Devotion is holy regulation, guiding hand and heart; a surrender of the self-will. . . . Devotion is the steady attraction of the soul towards one luminous object."[40] A regularized worship, fraught as it is with the temptation to laziness, nonetheless gives us a sense of continuity with others in the same tradition and with history.

Martineau recognized a clash between order and dignity on one hand and caprice and uncertainty on the other, and he sought to combine a free ritual with an ordered worship. He reflected on some of the advantages of a prayer book: it would unite the worshipper with others using the same resource; phrases as they became familiar could project a sense of the sacred; a liturgy could be created that that would fit into the theology of Unitarianism without stifling the spirit. He still had some reservations, however: "As in literature and art, so in religion, thought and affection need something more than self-repetition; they demand some freshness of movement."[41] Martineau disliked the Anglican prayer book, but he ultimately decided the concept of a prayer book was valid. Prayer books could help ministers focus their messages, help the liturgy remain poetic, and help the congregation establish liturgical ritual that fosters sense of community.

Thus Martineau wrestled with the task of composing a prayer book that would combine the beauty and dignity of a high liturgical worship with the simplicity of Unitarian theology. Martineau admired the Anglican liturgy, but he objected to its Trinitarian theology and the many references to divine wrath, which contradicted Martineau's own idea of a merciful and loving God. He thought that the idea of worship as a continual repetition was cold and limited. He respected the dignity and the historic value of the *Book of Common Prayer*, but he could not forgive it for killing prophecy and spontaneity: "Sweep it from the earth, replies prophetic hope, for it smothers the conscience, & makes the presence of the Most High a piece of ancient history."[42]

Common Prayer for Christian Worship, edited by Martineau, was published in 1862 and republished several times. The Preface and the last two services, numbers nine and ten, were by Martineau; in the rest of the work, he used existing orders of service and added Psalms and prayers from a variety of sources. He did not acknowledge his own authorship of these services in *Common Prayer*, but he did so later in his collection *Home Prayers, With Two Services for Public Worship*, in which the two services were reprinted. In his preface to *Common Prayer*, Martineau wrote, "the object of this collection was to preserve a rich treasury of devotion suited to both public and private use. . . ."[43]

The theme of *Common Prayer* is praise and trust in God. Martineau made generous use of biblical language and imagery, presenting God as a loving Father whom we approach as disciples of Christ. The ninth and tenth services convey the impression of a person awed by the majesty of God's presence among us. They are services of praise, not of dread. They stress our humility and the nearness of God. A typical prayer reads:

> Dearly beloved brethren, God, in whom we live and move and have our being, never leaves us, day or night. . . . Entering here, therefore, we cross the threshold of eternal things, and commune with the Father who seeth in secret. Let us shake off the dust of transitory care, and every disguise that can come between us and God: and, remembering whose disciples we are, come to the simplicity, though it should be also to the sorrows, of Christ.[44]

Martineau used his considerable talents, both literary and spiritual, to devise prayers and responses that spoke to the finest traditions of the Christian conscience, and especially the dissenting tradition, which until then had had no suitable substitute for the Anglican *Book of Common Prayer*. The merit of his efforts can be seen by the continued use of his prayer book into our own day. His prayers and responses have been adopted into many Protestant hymnals and have been used by both congregations and individuals. In *Common Prayer*, Martineau gave careful directions for worship, including chants and responses by the congregation, and suggestions about when to use readings and extemporaneous prayers. He also explained why he omitted services for certain parts of the Christian year, such as Lent: "it is considered better to leave each individual to the thoughts and feelings awakened by the approach of Good Friday and Easter, than to prescribe formal preparation, extending over a set period."[45]

Martineau wanted to retain the Unitarian connection with the Christian tradition, and accordingly all the prayers are addressed to God, as Martineau said was the practice of Christ, though such phrases as "Thy beloved, true, and glorified Son," "the love of Christ," and "through the knowledge of God, and of Jesus Christ our Lord" are used commonly. Horton Davies says of *Common Prayer*: "[Martineau's] real genius . . . is to be found in the freshness of an authentic first-hand experience of God felicitously phrased, and in the range of his moods of prayer ranging from the awed humility of his prayer of contrition and the mystical sense of the Communion of Saints to the prophetic insight of his Intercession for the Nation."[46] Davies considered Martineau's work to be an important development:

> The liturgical watershed for nineteenth century Unitarianism is the year 1862, when first appeared Common Prayer for Christian Worship, a formulary which combined the best of the older tradition in the first eight forms of service and in the orders for the two Sacraments, and which also expressed in the preface and in the remarkable ninth and tenth orders the genius of Martineau and the new Unitarian spirit and ethos which he exemplified with such distinction.[47]

Davies says of the ninth and tenth services that they "demonstrate his inventiveness in technique as well as in content. He is adept at producing new Canticles by collating Scriptural passages, as he is at providing new responses to prayers."

Common Prayer was used extensively and was republished many times; Davies has identified 40 editions.[48] Waller writes, ". . . in Martineau, Nonconformity produced a liturgical editor of rare genius for the first time."[49] *Common Prayer* and *Home Prayers* had a strong and lasting effect on Unitarianism. A further collection of Martineau's prayers, *Prayers in the Congregation and College*, published posthumously in 1911, vividly conveys awe in the presence of mystery, the majesty and holiness of God, who is also merciful. Martineau's prayers are still used in Unitarian churches, and his hymns are sung widely.

4. Rites

Martineau knew how easily worship becomes cold and imitative, separate from true human life. Yet the forms persist, he believed, because they have added meaning to our spiritual search. Rituals can preserve the venerable traditions that help us deal with the constant problems of sickness, death, sorrow, marriage, birth, and all forms of grief, joy, and disappointment. Martineau sought to relate the larger Christian tradition to the individual through a meaningful liturgy.

A. Baptism and Christening

Martineau used only two rites as part of regular worship: baptism (though he did not use that term) and the Lord's Supper, which he most often called "Communion." Of course, he performed weddings, funerals, and ordinations and had no difficulties with them, but he shared the Dissenters' reservations about the sacramental value of such rites. He did not believe them to be instruments of grace, though he thought they possessed important symbolic value.

Nor did Martineau believe baptism should be Trinitarian. He said that of the apostles only Paul was baptized, and he was baptized simply "into Christ Jesus."[50] Martineau also cited Romans 6.3[51] and added:

> Yet the tripersonal form, unhistorical as it is, is actually insisted on as essential by almost every Church in Christendom, and, if you have not had it pronounced over you, the ecclesiastical authorities cast you out as a heathen man, and will accord to you neither Christian recognition in your life, nor Christian burial in your death. It is a rule which would condemn as invalid every recorded baptism performed by an apostle; for if the book of Acts may be trusted, the invariable usage was baptism "in the name of Christ Jesus," and not "in the name of the Father, and of the Son, and of the Holy Spirit."[52]

Martineau distinguished baptism (a symbol of conversion or of joining the church) from the christening of infants. He thought baptism was suitable for those converted to Christianity from non-Christian religions but he spoke harshly of its use in other cases: "The [Anglican] clergy are habitually employed to perform a rite [baptism] on whose efficacy no one has the faintest reliance."[53] He refused to have his own children baptized but used a dedication service instead. He wrote his own "christening" service, based on Mark 10.16, which did not use water. In this service, which he used from 1850 to 1871, the child was dedicated to God with the following words: "I dedicate thee [name] to serve with thy whole mind the pure will of God; and offer thee, at the threshold of a Christian discipline, to be led by the hand of Jesus Christ into the kingdom of heaven."[54] To the parents he said, "You now present this child to be dedicated to God, & placed under the sanctifying hand of your gracious Master. . . . If I read aright the purpose of your hearts, you will endeavour to unfold & preserve in this child that pure & reverential mind whereof Christ said that 'of such is the kingdom of heaven.'"[55]

Martineau made clear in the service that the rite had nothing to do with a cleansing of original sin by saying to the parents, "You will guard from injury those native traces of docility & truthfulness & open love which recommended to our Lord the childish heart as the pure emblem of the kingdom of heaven."[56] He reasoned that the doctrine of original sin presumed that we are sinners by nature and that we are predetermined to that corrupt state. Yet the gospels and the writings of Paul, argued Martineau, assume that we have moral liberty, that we can know right from wrong and choose between them. The burden of working out redemption is laid on us, and we are capable of responding to the demands of justice.

By similar reasoning Martineau rejected the doctrine of vicarious atonement. Baptism does not wash away our sins, nor does Christ remove them through a rite. On the contrary, Martineau said, "Transference of guilt from one individual to another . . . involves a contradiction of the first principle of morals."[57] The concept of responsibility requires us to accept the consequences of our actions. Martineau pointed out the injustice of the British practices of substitionary punishment in the penal system and of hiring a substitute to go to war in one's own place. It violates morality, he said, to avoid the penalty of one's own acts or to shift the consequences onto someone else.

On the other hand, Martineau recognized the reality of sin. He said that to think of sin as due only to ignorance, social convention, or opinion overlooks the deliberate ways in which we separate ourselves from God. One might as well tell those who are guilty of wrong that all they have to do is take a different view of their actions, and they are thereby set free from the consequences. That, he said, is like telling a collapsed paralytic that all he must do is get up and run and he will be well.[58] Sin is a deliberate act and must be avoided by overcoming temptation and doing God's will. And ritual, Martineau believed, reinforces our determination to achieve the good.

Martineau saw the parents as surrogates for God and laid on them a heavy responsibility in the text he commonly used for christenings: "For a while you will constitute your child's religion; & when his spirit passes upward from the earthly to the heavenly stage of reverence, & bows before the heavenly Father, it will be with such conceptions of his wisdom & goodness as you have inspired, & with such tenderness & trust as you have evoked towards yourselves."[59] He believed parents must impart morality to their children and recognize the importance of their own example and teachings.

B. Communion

Martineau's views on christening were plain, but his use of the Lord's Supper was inconsistent.[60] In a sermon on St. Paul and the sacraments, preached at Paradise Street, Liverpool, on April 4, 1841 and again at Little Portland Street Chapel, London, on June 21, 1863, he said, "while the significance of baptism has quite ceased, the essential idea of the Lord's Supper remains undisturbed and in full force."[61] Later in his career, however, he said that the Lord's Supper was intended to go on only a few years until the expected return of the Lord. Nevertheless, he recognized its symbolic value and continued to celebrate it and even published Communion Addresses,[62] as for example at the opening of Manchester College in Oxford on October 19, 1893.

To better determine the role communion should play in worship, Martineau examined its origin, when the disciples joined Christ during his great humiliation, thus testifying that the core of Christianity is self-sacrifice. Martineau traced the history of the Lord's Supper through its transformation ("degeneration," he called it[63]) from a remembrance to a sacrament. The change, he said, came through time with the realizations that Christ would not return soon and that the rite was not an antidote to death, "the medicament of immortality," as Ignatius called it.[64] The change in understanding of the rite came, according to Martineau, when

> With the enlargement of its boundaries, the semi-communistic feeling of the first age wore away, the differences of social station made themselves felt, and the fraternal supper became rarer, and at last was dropped: the memorial distribution of the bread and wine being alone preserved, and erected into an independent rite. It was a gradual change, stealing on from place to place: but by the end of the second century was apparently pretty complete.[65]

In the beginning, Martineau said, the supper was a remembrance of Jesus by those who had known him personally. They wanted to preserve their living contact with him as his disciples and assistants in his ministry, and this meal provided symbolic access to him and preserved their relationship to their teacher. When the group, having been dispersed after Calvary, reunited at Jerusalem or other places, naturally they would want to restore the connection so recently severed. By reenacting their last meal with Jesus, even when only the two elements were shared, his followers could assuage the sorrow they had experienced on that last night with him.

For Martineau, in the parts that remind us of self-denial, Communion requires that, as a key to religion, we reject pride and self-assertion. Its value is that it forces on us the understanding that life is not meant for pleasant living under the lightest possible burden, nor is happiness the goal. Our lives are broken, but through communion with God we find redemption. Communion aims to make us whole.

Martineau objected to the Church of England's concept of Holy Communion because he did not believe a ceremony could either change God's will or alter human nature. Communion in his thinking was a commemoration, open to anyone who wanted to renew a connection with God. Its effectiveness depended not on any miraculous change in the bread and wine, nor even on ingesting them, but on the sincere desire to join with the spirit of Christ in renewal. Frances Cooke, a member of Hope Street Church during Martineau's ministry, described his communion in her memoir of him. She wrote, presumably quoting him:

> The chief feature of the rite of Communion, is that it identifies the disciples with their Master in his moment of utter humiliation and surrender, and so bears witness to the great truth that the very essence and crown of our religion is self-sacrifice. . . . We cannot embrace his cross and yet refuse our own. We cannot raise the cup of his remembrance to our lips without a secret pledge to him, to one another, to the great company of faithful in every age, that we, too, hold ourselves at God's disposal, that we will ask nothing on our own account, that we will pass simply into the Divine hand to take us whither it will.[66]

Communion may have been symbolic instead of sacramental for Martineau, but it was nonetheless an important observance. He offered Communion as part of the Confirmation service for the young, to symbolize their moving away from the closed circle of the home into the larger world of untried responsibilities. Thus they participate in and join the historic church. The communion is a rite of remembrance and a wish to become part of the great body of devoted seekers, the true Church of God. Martineau prepared the young by holding weekly classes, during which he taught them of the development of the Lord's Supper. The young people were invited to ask questions and criticize. When the course ended, they would gather on a Sunday morning for a sermon and Communion service.

Martineau believed that, in his form of the communion, he was following what Jesus intended:

> Though he cannot have promised to put himself, corporeally or incorporeally, into any sacramental bread or wine taken in his name, he may have desired, when the world would not listen to him, that they should not forget him, but when, as now, they brake bread and passed the cup together, should remember with what thankful blessing he sent these symbols round, and should read in them and draw out of them all the meaning of his living presence.[67]

The Lord's Supper on its first occasion was both a Jewish festival of Passover and a social meal by the close-knit band. The occasion was a spiritual crisis combining both danger and farewell. It was their last Passover, their last gathering. Naturally, they would want an unbroken tie to their teacher: "Here was no new rite, but merely an assumed continuance of a community of life begun."[68]

In sum, Martineau believed that ritual, if used thoughtfully and effectively, provides help in our spiritual and moral growth. We are brought closer to God: "Devotion is the steady attraction of the soul towards one luminous object."[69] Rituals and prayer book can help us persevere by association with phrases and ideas that have been hallowed by time and by use by other people searching in the same way. Yet we need to avoid mere repetition and retain freshness of thought and affection—to preserve our inheritance and our freedom to go beyond it.

5. Elements of Worship
A. Hymns

Hymns were an important part of worship for Martineau, yet he found much to criticize in the approach of the Unitarians of his day to hymns. They used hymns from a variety of traditions, but often in what he considered a careless manner. The hymns were not matched with the liturgy, and the hymnals often did not have enough "occasional" hymns for specific occasions. Martineau, in contrast, sought to avoid this unfocused, "cafeteria" approach to worship. Further, Martineau deplored the influence of rationalism, which "checked these creations of piety, and dragged genius from the altar."[70]

For Martineau, hymns combined the finest emotions with lofty metaphor and imagery. Hymns are a special kind of poetry: prayer set to music. Martineau once described poetry as "the pure outpouring of any human emotion that is natural and graceful."[71] In singing hymns, he believed, we join with each other and with the great ones of the ages in approaching God. Early on, Martineau developed a love of music that he retained throughout his life. He considered music an important means of access to the Divine. According to Craufurd, "Insensibly it [music] counteracted the depressing influence of his old indwelling Deism. In sober truth, poetry and music were to him what Emerson called 'liberating Gods.'"[72]

Martineau recognized that hymns have a strong influence on the beliefs of the church. Sermons are heard and then reinforced or replaced with other sermons, and so with prayers. But hymns, by repetition, become part of a person's whole religious sense. Hymns learned in youth continue their influence into maturity. A congregation that sings hymns together develops a similar religious outlook. Hymns thus may have an influence greater than that of a denomination's officials or publications. Brown suggests, "To understand the real breadth and depth of a movement's beliefs, it is often better to go firstly to its hymnal, even before reading its sermons or academic theology. . . . They are more suited to evoking general religious emotions and the creation of religious atmosphere than they are able to define any single, clear doctrinal position."[73]

Martineau himself wrote three hymns. "Thy way is in the deep, O Lord!," written in 1840, describes the fears and storms that test and tempt us. In the hymn, God responds to sincere prayer, and our faith will bring us victory by dispelling grief and wiping away tears. "A Voice upon the Midnight Air" (composition date unknown) describes the sorrows of Christ, his agony and martyrdom. From the cross he imparts blessings to us, and in good time we shall make that same lone journey. "'Where is your God?' They Say" dates to 1873 and reflects Martineau's mature thought. It describes God as within the soul, responsive as a friend: God is not external, "in moving cloud," "flashing storm," or "thunder," but internal, "in silent high desire," "wakening love," and "wonder, duty grown divine." Sorrows are shadows of God's will, "sad messengers of God," he said in another place.[74] If we come to God with humility and listen for the still small voice, then "broken love's made whole,/And saddened hearts rejoice."

Martineau also adapted two hymns from John Milton. While the main ideas are Milton's, we may infer that they also represent Martineau's thought, since otherwise he would not have used them. "How Lovely Are Thy Dwellings, Lord" stresses the need for complete trust in and reliance on God; God is always near to the just and righteous. "The Lord Will Come, and Not Be Slow" stresses the greatness and majesty of God. The Kingdom of God will come on earth when truth springs from us, and God is the righteous judge who redresses wrongs.

Martineau compiled three hymnals, two of which had wide circulation and influence. The first, *A Collection of Hymns for Christian Worship* (1831), consists of 273 hymns. The second, *Hymns for the Christian Church and Home* (1840), compiled while he was minister in Liverpool, contains Martineau's first two hymns. According to John Julian's *Dictionary of Hymnology*, it "was quickly recognised as pre-eminent among the (hymn) books in use among the non-subscribing churches."[75] Martineau's third hymnal, *Hymns of Praise and Prayer* (1873), also contains his first two hymns.

A Collection of Hymns for Christian Worship

Martineau said that this 1831 collection was designed for the use of a congregation whose worship "is paid solely to the God and Father of our Lord and Saviour Jesus Christ."[76] None of his hymns was included among the 273, but he did use five by his sister, Harriet. He also included 60 by Isaac Watts. It was compiled explicitly for his church in Dublin but was used there only briefly. It was not used outside of his Dublin church and had little influence in the movement, though it laid the groundwork for his further reflections on hymns.

In selecting and editing hymns for his collection, Martineau struggled over the question of which alterations were permissible, for he did not want to abuse the intent of a hymn's author. He wrote in the preface, "While it has been an object to avoid all frivolous deviations from the original compositions of the several authors, it has not been thought necessary to abandon hymns prevailingly excellent, when an alteration seemed to correct passages objectionable on the ground either of theology or of taste."[77] Following these guidelines, he altered 30 of the hymns. The hymnal prints both the original line and his alterations. Most, though not all, of the changes were minor. In the following examples, the original line is first.

> Awake, ye saints! And raise your eyes;
>   Christians! Awake, and raise your eyes;
>
> Father of all! in every age
>   Father of all, whose cares extend
>
> Greatest of beings! Source of life!
>   Great cause of all things! Source of life!
>
> My dear Redeemer and my Lord!
>   I read my duty in thy word

Although Martineau claimed that all of his changes in hymns were minor,[78] some of them appear to be major, as when he omitted verses or substituted his own verses. For example, verse five of "Awake, My Soul, Stretch Every Nerve" reads in Doddridge's original:

> Blest Saviour, introduced by thee,
>   Have I my Race begun;
> And crown'd with Victory at thy feet
>   I'll lay mine Honours down.

Martineau substituted:

> My soul! With sacred ardour fired,
>   The glorious prize pursue;
> And meet with joy the high command
>   To bid this earth adieu![79]

We can question why Martineau made such changes but then called his alterations minor. Perhaps he did not consider substituting verses the same as making line-by-line alterations, which generally were, indeed, minor. He also said he altered words that over a long time had so changed their meaning that the author's intent was lost by the original words, his alterations thus being designed to more nearly preserve the original intent.[80] Perhaps the apparently major line-by-line changes can be attributed to this reasoning.

Hymns for the Christian Church and Home

Julian's *Dictionary of Hymnology* describes *Hymns for the Christian Church and Home* (1840), which Martineau wrote while he was minister at Paradise Street Chapel in Liverpool, as "the book which has made the most striking epoch in the history of Unitarian hymnody."[81] It became the most widely used Unitarian hymnal of its day and had a strong effect on worship in the churches.

In the preface to that hymnal, Martineau said the special function of hymns is to raise the thoughts of people from the ordinary to the divine through the combined use of poetry and music cast in the form of prayer. The words are taken from the great poets, and the music uses the genius of composers such as Haydn or Spohr to raise us from "our own puny dreams."

> It is easy to perceive on what principle of selection a compiler
> of hymns must proceed, who is impressed with this idea of the

relation between poetry and worship. His rule will be, simply to take those poems which appear to shed forth, with the greatest genuineness and force, the emotions of a mind possessed with the religious or mysterious conception of God, of life and death, of duty, of futurity.[82]

Martineau chose hymns with consideration for the sensitivity of worshippers accustomed to the hymns of their youth, hymns that had affected their beliefs. In this collection, unlike his first one, he was reluctant to alter the hymns, and he was careful about introducing too many new ones. He did not want to disturb or bring pain to the sensitivities of faithful worshipers. He also tried to avoid bias based on his personal belief but labored instead to attend to the devotional needs of the congregations. He wrote, "It is not the business of a hymn-book editor either to relax or to overstrain the dependence of religious feeling on historical association; but to provide a voice for actual affections, neither leaving them behind by saying too much, nor failing to bear them aloft by a breath too faint and feeble."[83]

Hymns of Praise and Prayer

Martineau retained his interest in worship, and particularly hymnody, throughout his career. Gradually he came to recognize that the changing culture, especially the growth of industry and technology, required some accommodation between tradition and the demands of a new time. He was a true conservative in that he wanted to retain the good of the past, and he would change only when there was a compelling reason to do so, not just for the sake of novelty.

In his 1873 hymnal *Hymns of Praise and Prayer*, Martineau again stated that he had been faithful to the original wording of the hymns except where noted, with the author's name given in italics if any change at all had been made. He included a special index for hymns in which the alteration was in the first line. He wrote, "Of mere arbitrary tampering with the materials which it is my duty and delight to touch with only a reverent hand, I trust no trace will be found."[84]

Martineau noted two opposing reasons for the new hymnal, issued 33 years after the previous one. First, he recognized the effects of the

Oxford Movement within the Established Church in the late 1830s, a movement characterized by a longing for an earlier piety that sought to recover important treasures of prayer and poetic devotion, and which "clings for strength to the last link in the catena [a series of connected things] of saintly examples."[85] Martineau criticized the Oxford Movement's tendency to give "exaggerated prominence . . . to the objective and mythological elements which have found their way into the faith of Christendom: simple and natural piety finds there no shelter and no voice."[86] Second, Martineau had observed an opposite tendency toward the loosening or expunging in hymnals of the sacred traditions, which he saw as a symptom of decline in an important tradition of piety.

To counteract those two tendencies, Martineau selected new hymns that stressed the inner life and omitted old hymns that "mainly dealt with objective incidents either in biblical history or in the apocalyptic representation of the future."[87] He thought hymns should focus less on historical incidents and more on directly inspiring the heart, helping people to move from concern about the past into concern about the future. One change resulting from this determination was that this third hymnal contained fewer hymns dealing with a general resurrection. That subject was of greater concern to people of an earlier generation, said Martineau, but "[t]ime has laid that question to rest, and dismissed the imagery of the general judgment to its place in the Messianic mythology; but other questions now occupy a similar position."[88]

Of the 797 hymns in Martineau's third hymnal, 417 were taken from his second hymnal, and 380 were newly added. The 255 authors represented every part of Christendom from Roman Catholic to Unitarian. This hymnal included two of Martineau's own, "'Where Is Your God?'" They Say" and "Thy Way Is in the Deep, O Lord!," and also the two that he adapted from Milton. All four hymns were listed as anonymous. A later hymnal by another compiler, *The Essex Hall Hymnal Revised* (published in 1902, after Martineau's death), includes these four hymns, as well as Martineau's earlier hymn "A Voice upon the Midnight Air," and gave him proper credit.In conclusion, Martineau's influence on hymnody has been mostly through his own surviving hymns. His reasoning behind compilation of the hymns has stood the test of time, and he led later Unitarians at least to reflect on working out a rationale for which hymns to use.

B. Prayer

In Martineau's theory of worship, hymnody was not the only important element to a successful experience—prayer was equally essential. Martineau's prayers are a form of conversation with God: "I would be understood to speak of a direct and mutual communion of spirit with spirit between ourselves and God, in which he receives our affection and gives a responsive breathing of his inspiration."[89] His prayers are to a personal God appealing for a change in our blindness, inconstancy, and excuses. They express shame over our lack of trust and failure of duty. They contain familiar petitions: to keep us from temptation, to help us bear our crosses with patience, and to help us realize our need for repentance. According to Martineau, prayer is the most familiar of several ways to approach God, and thus it plays a key role in worship. Prayer occurs in numerous forms during worship: invocation, confession, intercession, and adoration. It varies according to its place in the liturgy, such as call to worship, offertory, sermon prayer, pastoral prayer, and benediction. Thus, said Martineau, the worshiper is afforded several chances to commune with God. Each kind of prayer has different characteristics, appealing in turn to the mind and the heart.

Prayer, according to Martineau, is prompted by both the awareness of sin and the vision of Perfect Holiness. It is a form of conversation with God beyond either speech or reason. In prayer all pretence and vanity are stripped away. The heart is the secret place of God. As we trust in God, we lose all fear; prayer reminds us that God is with us. Martineau valued reason, and he said prayer must not violate reason—that is, it should not be irrational. But prayer is fundamentally an outpouring of the spirit utilizing not only such emotions as joy and love, so that our potential becomes clear to us, but also shame and sin, to remind us of our failures before God. The end of both kinds of emotion is to renew the spirit by connecting us with God.

In his prayers, Martineau sought union with God, the source of truth, love, and righteousness; in other words, he sought to become Christ-like. He pleaded with God for conversion from base desires to the higher call of the Spirit. He prayed for "the simplicity of Christ. . . . Let the divine image of the Son of God visit us with power."[90] Only the pure in heart, he says, can see God, and he recounts the sins that separate us from God: "the wandering desire, the vain fancy, the scornful doubt, the untrustful care, unruly passions, hardness of heart," and bitterness.[91] Through prayer we find strength to turn from our guilty ways. We come to God with gratitude, to resolve the turmoil and anxiety of life. The reward of prayer is peace of conscience.

Martineau's prayers are direct petitions to God without the intercession of Christ. Yet he counted himself fully Christian in his prayers, believing he followed Christ's example, and his prayers contain many references to Christ. He prayed to be like Christ, filled with divine humility and simplicity; "May the same mind be in us which was also in Jesus Christ"[92] is a common plea.

Of the 70 prayers that were examined for the present work, 41 refer to Christ; 29 do not. Of his three benedictions in *Services for Public Worship*, two refer to Christ. His prayers are addressed to God the Father, not to Christ, though he uses such petitions as "We commend ourselves to thee, in the faith of Christ our Lord" and "hold us all to the pure fidelity of Christ."[93] References to Christ occur mostly at the end of the prayers, subordinate to the main thrust. Perhaps the references are placed at the end to remind the congregation that they are attending Christian worship. His prayers do not use Christ as an authority or intermediary; Martineau prays with Christ, not through him. Prayers remind us that we are part of the Christian family and that we are fellow-worshipers with Christ.

Martineau's theology of prayer, like his thoughts on hymnody, was a response to two opposite currents of thought in England. On the one hand, Martineau believed that the orthodox were too rigid in their theology and did not allow the spirit to flow freely. On the other hand, Martineau sought to oppose the necessitarians, or positivists, who argued against the value of prayer by insisting that only that which appeals to the senses or can be known through the study of nature has validity. Martineau sought a middle ground. He knew that prayer is often abused by people who attribute too much to it—assuming prayer can alter the course of nature and bring rain or stop hurricanes—as well as by those who put it aside as unscientific and beyond our knowledge.

Martineau was well schooled in science and believed that the universe is governed by fixed natural laws. Some say that because of these natural laws, prayer is self-deceiving and can accomplish nothing. Yet Martineau held to his faith that we still can have personal intercourse with God, that we can place ourselves under his will, and that God in turn is open to our appeal. He solved the problem thus: "We must accommodate ourselves to the stern mechanism of God's natural and unmoral laws; and then he will succor us, not by altering them, but by inspiring us,—by lifting us to bear their burthen,—by throwing open to us the almightiness of his companionship and the shelter of his love."[94]

Martineau's prayers are not sectarian, and they had a strong influence on the free churches of England, and even beyond. Other denominations have used his prayers, and they are found in modern Unitarian sources. They continue to be used widely in worship books and hymnals, though his sermons are not often read and his books not often used. According to Davies,

> Whether acknowledged or unacknowledged, Martineau's prayers have become a notable part of the currency of prayer in English devotional life. Their only defect is that, an irritating didacticism although usually submerged, occasionally emerges to defect the attention from God to man.
>
> When a liturgical genius like Martineau writes modern classics of prayer his influence is bound to be profound. This can be seen in the . . . Orders of Public Worship for use in the Chapel of Manchester College, and [Martineau] became the leader of English Unitarians of his day.[95]

Martineau's widest influence, however, was felt in the ranks of the other Free churches in England. Many of Martineau's prayers warrant ecumenical usage.[96] In fact, Martineau's prayers continue to be used today. The Unitarian Universalist Christian published a collection of 15 prayers in 1984,[97] and the Orders of Worship noted by Davies is still used at Harris Manchester College and in other Unitarian churches. His prayers are found in *Hymns of the Spirit*, published in the United States in 1937 and still in use.

Meaningful prayer is essential to religion, said Martineau, and worship is incomplete without it. If we do not acknowledge our reliance on God, religion is no more than tradition. If we do not avail ourselves of direct intercourse between the human mind and the Divine, we throw aside a valuable part of our religion, which then becomes at most a sentimental remnant, like the grin on Alice's Cheshire cat. Without prayer, we turn away from God: "Religion is no more possible without prayer, than poetry without language, or music without atmosphere."[98] As long as we avail ourselves of prayer, life retains its hope and meaning, and we are reminded that we are not alone, that the world possesses realities greater than meet the eye or than science can investigate. We become part of an unseen world. Prayer is not the cry of the defeated but a recognition by the strong: "He who prays is at the beginning of aspiration, not at the evaporating end of impulse: he is drawn, not driven: he is not painting himself upon vacancy, but is surrendering himself to a Presence real and everlasting."[99]

C. Sermons

In the traditional churches, sermons are expositions of scripture and doctrine. Martineau relied on that model to some extent, but also added new innovations.

For Martineau, the sermon was an integral part of worship, supported by and supporting the prayers and hymns, although not the primary part of the worship. He felt an urgent need to awaken and reinforce our divine mission and to fight against all that deters us from our relation with God: doubts, false doctrines, the lure of ease, "that poisonous notion of enjoyment as the end of life, which in so many men absolutely stifles the higher soul,"[100] and the distractions of science and trade. Sermons, he believed, are needed to awaken us from the trends that lure us back to our animal nature with the promise that we will thereby be relieved from the challenges of our higher nature: "The [religious] reformer's work is always the same, to remove these mediatorial obstructions; to revert to the living Mind of the Eternal; to tear away the thick disguise of dead custom; to scatter the murky clouds that shut in with their damp curtain the immeasurable heavens; & present the Conscience naked and solitary to the awful thrill of God."[101] In so doing, Martineau sought to appeal to the intellect and the affection by combining reason with his insights into what he felt was God's will.

Martineau's sermons were mostly pastoral, designed to bring people into closer relation with God, to show them the path to righteous living, and to help them develop their spiritual life. His sermons often dealt with personal problems such as grief and loneliness. He helped people to see themselves as children of God and to understand the meaning of godliness and how God dwells in us. Generally, he thought sermons should be biblical expositions: "The preacher's function . . . is to take out of Scripture some thought so little entangled with conditions of time and place as already to speak for itself, and thence to transfer it unchanged to his hearer's experience and duties in their different time and place."[102]

Throughout his career, Martineau maintained a high standard of thought and eloquence in his sermons. They contain flowing prose and many brilliant epigrams. As was common in the 19th century, many of his sentences are long and complex. They must have been hard to follow and certainly would have required the close attention of the hearer. Even more difficult than the prose style, however, was the deep philosophical thought in so many of the sermons. He never resorted to humor of any kind, not even irony, because he considered the liturgy and all its parts to be a sacred undertaking, and he wanted no digression or distraction. He was determined that sermons should teach us of holiness and reveal God as the source of holiness, thus reclaiming for us our divine heritage.

A few of his sermons are more like philosophical treatises, such as "Time, Nature, God, and the Soul," which deals with the relation of God and nature to the concept of time. "The Sphere and Spirit of Faith" and "Faith the Symbolic Aspect of Truth" are lectures on the nature and development of faith. "The Unjust Steward" is mostly an explanation of Roman culture in the time of Jesus, without a strong pastoral purpose. "In Him We Live and Move and Have our Being" is a discourse comparing several theories of God. Such sermons are few and can be considered aberrations, such as all ministers have in their collections. In addition to dealing with philosophical topics, some of his sermons, especially earlier in his career, are rigorous examinations of the text and the historical setting without personal application.

Although Martineau often reflected on philosophical and intellectual issues, he tried to avoid references to the political or social circumstances of his day in his sermons. He never discussed politics, economics, or social reform in sermons, though he did so frequently in lectures and articles. Because his sermons did not discuss current issues, they retain their freshness and can be read today without loss of meaning. He did not urge doctrine, Unitarian or other, but sought to show people how to find God, duty, and joy in their hearts.

In composing his sermons, Martineau's active mind found inspiration in an unusual variety of disciplines. The use of science to illustrate religious truth, for example, was not common. But Martineau had an extensive knowledge of botany, biology, astronomy, physics, anthropology, and the debates over evolution, and he frequently used references to and examples from science in his sermons. In addition, he was one of the early and strong proponents of the new discipline of biblical criticism. He made use of the best biblical scholarship and often employed it in explaining a text.

Although his congregations were small, Martineau's sermons achieved a lasting influence through his five printed collections.[103] The Rev. Robert Collyer tells us that Martineau preached to a small number of habitual attendees and casual visitors, though his sermons were read by a much greater number.[104] Frances Power Cobbe, a member of Martineau's church in Little Portland Street Chapel, London, offers one explanation for the small size of his congregation:

> It was a perpetual and tantalising enigma to the regular attendants in Little Portland-street Chapel, how it happened that men and women, ostensibly capable of appreciating Dr. Martineau's sermons, so often put in an appearance once or twice and never returned. The explanation which commends itself to me is that such good people listened to the great preacher in a somewhat

distracted state of mind, having expected his discourse to fall into one or other of certain familiar categories, and, finding it impossible to pigeon-hole them according to their anticipations, they went away sorrowful. . . .[105]

Cobbe described Martineau as grave, with calm eloquence, and entirely unaffected in the pulpit. She said he never assumed the tone of prophet, priest, or professor; nor did he seem to want to win people over to any position of his, or to turn them away from loyalty to any other church. She also, however, explained that he might be hard to follow:

> I have often compared the experience of listening to one of Dr. Martineau's sermons to the invigoration of a walk over a mountain. There was at the outset the effort—often considerable—to climb the steep and slippery ascent. Then came the breath of purer, keener air, and freer movement; then the outlook over wider horizons, sometimes grand and solemn, sometimes sweet and restful. Finally there was the pause of prayer and adoration on the summit.[106]

Martineau's sermons fit into his general plan of worship. They were thoughtful and carefully constructed and made use of lofty metaphor. They were precise, they followed the best thinking of both philosophy and theology, and yet they were not pedantic. Martineau generally dealt with concerns of the congregation, celebrating the seasons, transitions of life, the joys and sorrows inherent in the human situation. In Martineau's view, sermons, like the other elements of worship, were intended to bring the congregant into closer communion with God.

Martineau's thoughts, however, were often more lofty than most people could grasp, though such a charge would have caused him chagrin. Craufurd noted that one of Martineau's sermons contained enough ideas for a dozen sermons by anyone else, which he considered a liability. Perhaps, he wrote, it is easier to read them than it was to hear them: "In fact Martineau's addresses are too full of ideas to be adequately comprehended when delivered from the pulpit; they need to be carefully thought over, in order that their power and beauty may be really appreciated."[107] Martineau knew his ideas were often beyond the understanding of most people, but he felt he had to be true to his own light. He would not have wanted to compromise his native instincts, even had he known how.

Martineau had specific goals in mind for his sermons. One function of sermons, he thought, is to give us direction by persuading conscience to challenge us, so that it will become "the master of our industry, the counsellor of our doubts, the victor of our temptations. And whether it be to write a history, to solve a problem, or to remedy an abuse, whoever has clearly before him such an end in view, sails with his compass alight through the wildest night, and, bearing onward, is heedless of the pelting rain, and unbewildered by the gloom."[108]

Martineau never used his sermons for argument or to engage in controversy. He wanted his sermons to be tools for calm and peace in what he saw as the intellectual ferment in the Christendom of his day. Intellectual disputes, he claimed, were never settled, just forgotten eventually.[109] He wanted his own sermons to support personal religion and the harmony of simple and natural piety.

Sermons, Martineau believed, should be "sacred thoughts," to quote the title of two of his volumes of sermons. They should be contemporary in the sense of speaking to the morals of the day, not to some other age, and should apply some firm or eternal standard. By appealing to such a standard, morals do not recede under the threat of relative ethics or changing mores. This standard should be both rational and revealed, that is, based on the will of God as demonstrated by Jesus and reconciled by reason. Sermons should relate to the whole of life, and the more complex our understanding of society and nature, the greater the challenge: "the more numerous are the keys on which the Divine touch may strike, and the fuller the chords through which the World will peal."[110] Sermons, Martineau believed, should not oversimplify life by picking at one part or another; rather, they should help us see a larger picture.

Martineau's sermons relied on the Bible; only rarely did he quote other sources. He said sermons should not be turned into lectures—a failing he recognized in himself. In an address to new ministers, he said: "Complaint is often made that the pulpit is turned into the Lecture desk; that criticism, evidences, metaphysics, history,—every husk that hangs about divine things rather than the living kernel, is offered to a craving people; they ask for bread, and we give them a stone. A thousand times have I owned the truth to myself, and been humbled by it."[111] That is, opinions on politics, science, exploration, or social movements belong in lectures, not sermons.

In his sermons, Martineau sought to encourage people by bringing them closer to the divinity within them. He wanted them to recognize the moral consequences of their religion, the duty incumbent on them as Christians trying to build the Kingdom of God. He was not a purveyor of palliatives. The metaphor of the Pharisee was ever in his mind: hypocrisy, he knew, is not within others only, but also among those who are smug about their religion and are grateful that they are possessors of a superior way, those whose prayers cause them to be overly confident of their intimacy with God instead of seeking a better way. Some, he said, are so satisfied with their worship that

> they believe in the power of devotional persuasion, and hold it to be the Christian's supreme accomplishment; and they are fond of declaring, in language which we cannot repeat without a shudder, that they will give the Lord no rest till he sends them what they want. . . . Intellect as well as faith has its Pharisees; and philosophy has been heard in the temple, thanking God that it is not as others, superstitious, idolaters, and Calvinists, and telling him with what invariable correctness it has learned to think of him and his government.[112]

Complacency is a close relative of pride, and Martineau saw the harm caused by the arrogance of excessively rational forms of worship, or by taking delight in identifying the fallacies of other people's creeds. Such negative attitudes, he believed, were not conducive to real religion.

In conclusion, Martineau believed in a personal and indwelling God. Worship, he believed, aims to strengthen our relation with God. Martineau avoided the utilitarian idea that worship is a means toward moral awareness and a sense of duty. Rather, he taught that in worship the soul returns home and gains deeper insight and holier aspirations. Worship develops the latent God within us and instructs us in conforming to the pattern of the good and holy, to the Divine Image. Morality and ethics are a consequence of worship but not the primary reason for it. Martineau came to believe worship should be regularized in form and content, so long as this does not impinge on the freedom of the spirit.

Notes

1. Jackson, 143.
2. Horton Davies, 265.
3. *Essays IV*, 378.
4. *Essays IV*, 488.
5. *Endeavours*, 138–39.
6. Preface, vii.
7. *Ibid.*, v.
8. *Ibid.*, v.
9. *Hours I*, 277–78.
10. *Hours II*, 337–39.
11. "The Doctrine of Punishment," 1.
12. *Ibid.*, 1.
13. *Studies*, xiv.
14. "What is Christianity? No. 11: Relation of Belief to Character," 8.
15. *Essays IV*, 378.
16. *Ibid.*.
17. Horton Davies, 268–69.
18. *Ibid*.
19. Carpenter, 443.
20. *Hours II*, 334.
21. "The Church of the Future," 10.
22. *Studies*, xiii–xiv.
23. *Hours II*, 335.
24. Smart (1972), 75.
25. *Studies*, xiii.
26. *Hours I*, 16.
27. *Studies*, 39.
28. Schneewind, 246.
29. "Communion Address at the opening of Manchester College Thursday, October 19, 1893," Proceedings and Addresses on the Occasion of the Opening of the College Buildings and Dedication of the Chapel, October 18–19, 1893, 29.
30. Waller, *James Martineau*, 340–41.
31. *Ibid.*, 341.
32. *Essays IV*, 438.

33. *Endeavours*, 181.
34. *Endeavours*, 181.
35. Letter to the Rev. Dr Sadler, minister of Rosslyn Hill Chapel, Hampstead, November 6, 1860, quoted in Drummond and Upton I, 383.
36. *Hours II*, 336.
37. *Hours I*, 182–83.
38. *Hymns for the Christian Church and Home, Collected and Edited by James Martineau*, vii.
39. *Hours I*, 81.
40. *Endeavours*, 391.
41. *Common Prayer for Christian Worship: in Ten Services for Morning and Evening, with Special Collects, Prayers, and Occasional Services*, vi.
42. "The Negative Faith," 10.
43. *Common Prayer for Christian Worship*, xii.
44. *Ibid*., tenth service.
45. *Ibid*., xii.
46. Horton Davies, 276.
47. *Ibid*., 271.
48. *Ibid*.
49. Waller, *James Martineau*, 280.
50. Acts 2.38.
51. "Do you not know that all of us who have been baptized into Christ Jesus were baptized into his death?"
52. *The Seat of Authority in Religion*, 516.
53. *Essays II*, 54.
54. "Christening Address," 2.
55. "Christening Address," 1.
56. *Ibid*., 3.
57. *The Seat of Authority in Religion*, 479.
58. *Endeavours*, 330.
59. "Christening Address," 4.
60. Craufurd, 106–7.
61. "St. Paul's Doctrine of the Church and the Sacraments," unpublished sermon quoted in Waller, *James Martineau*, 251.
62. Craufurd, 106–7.
63. *The Seat of Authority in Religion*, 541.
64. *Ibid*., 540.
65. *Ibid*., 540–41.
66. *In Memoriam James Martineau, 1805–1900*, 31. It is not clear in the original whether Cooke is directly quoting Martineau, but the similarity of this passage to the one cited in note 89 makes this a reasonable assumption.
67. *The Seat of Authority in Religion*, 530–31.
68. *Ibid*., 531.

69. "The Realm of Order," 391.
70. *Hymns for the Christian Church and Home*, vi.
71. "The Negative Faith," 12.
72. Craufurd, 16.
73. Brown, *James Martineau*, 16.
74. "The Faith of Suffering," 5.
75. Julian, 716.
76. *A Collection of Hymns for Christian Worship*, v.
77. *Ibid.*, iii.
78. His complete statement reads: "If there are any deviations from the originals which appear not to receive defence from either of these pleas of theological or of metrical necessity, they will be found referable to the change which time gradually makes in the meaning of words, and the force of imagery. In a very few instances, phrases once dignified or affecting, and now confessedly mean, or even ludicrous, have been exchanged for others more truly expressive of the author's real feelings. But in every case, the standard to which the editor has endeavoured to conform has been, not the sentiment which he would have liked the poet to express, but that which he conceives the poet actually wished to express, and which, till the religious dialect of his day began to play him false, he succeeded in expressing" (*Hymns for the Christian Church and Home*, xi). In another hymnal he wrote: "Deviations from the original texts have been kept down to the lowest possible amount; and, unless occasionally imposed by metrical necessity, admitted only for grave reasons of religious veracity. Of mere arbitrary tampering with the materials which it is my duty and delight to touch with only a reverent hand, I trust no trace will be found" (*Hymns of Praise and Prayer*, xvii–xviii).
79. *A Collection of Hymns for Christian Worship*, No. 194.
80. *Hymns for the Christian Church and Home*, xi.
81. Julian, 1194.
82. *Hymns for the Christian Church and Home*, viii.
83. *Hymns of Praise and Prayer*, xii.
84. *Ibid.*, xviii.
85. *Ibid.*, vi.
86. *Ibid.*, vii.
87. *Ibid.*, x.
88. *Ibid.*, xiii.
89. *Hours II*, 224.
90. *Ibid.*, 8, 10.
91. *Ibid.*, 16.
92. *Ibid.*, 17.
93. *Ibid.*, 30, 32.
94. *Hours II*, 231.
95. Horton Davies, 278.
96. See, for example, John Hunter's *Devotional Services*. Horton Davies notes (p. 281) that

many of Martineau's prayers are included in W. E. Orchard's *Divine Service* and in *The Free Church Book of Common Prayer.*
97. *Unitarian Universalist Christian*, Spring/Summer 1984, 5–16.
98. *Ibid.*, 236.
99. *Essays IV*, 488.
100. *Essays IV*, 451.
101. *The Negative Faith*, 11.
102. "Memorial Preface," in Thom, *A Spiritual Faith*, xxi.
103. *Endeavours After the Christian Life* (1892); *Hours of Thought on Sacred Things, A Volume of Sermons* (1876); *Hours of Thought on Sacred Things. Second Series* (1880); *National Duties and Other Sermons and Addresses* (1903); *Studies of Christianity* (1858).
104. Collyer, 74.
105. *Ibid.*, 31.
106. *Ibid.*, 33.
107. Craufurd, 4.
108. *Hours I*, 142.
109. Preface to *Hours II*, iii.
110. *Essays IV*, 72.
111. *National Duties*, 458.
112. *National Duties*, 150–52.

Chapter III:
Martineau's Concept of the Ministry

1. The Nature of the Ministry

Martineau believed that the Christian ministry was the highest form of service to humanity. He devoted his life to the ministry, both as the leader of congregations and in his roles as teacher and Principal of Manchester College. He sought to strengthen the ministry, which he felt had declined both in the public eye and in quality. Worship, he said, was the obvious and most important function of the minister, and he lamented the decline in the liturgical tradition.

Martineau believed the ministry had been weakened partly because it was ill defined. Ministers were expected to be public speakers, encouragers of popular causes, and socialites. Too much is expected from ministers, he said, and they in turn expect too much from themselves.

Martineau believed a professional ministry would help improve the public perception of ministers. It seemed to him that the public of his day saw the ministry as less important than in an earlier day; the pulpit was no longer the sole, or even the most important, disseminator of ideas. Newspapers, he said, were now the main force in molding minds. Although the clergy had once dominated public morality and thought, now that function had been taken over by universities or by "the moneyed classes":

> it is their will, their morality, their sentiments, that now constitute the largest ingredient in public opinion, and impress upon events the course which they should take. . . . Prosperity is their idol; the spread of luxury, the multiplication of external refine-

ments, their measure of civilization; the cheapness of food and clothing, their criterion of a nation's happiness; the tendency to produce wealth, their prevailing standard of utility. By this test they estimate the worth of mental and moral qualities; the education that will tell upon the purse is indeed essential; of that which only unfolds the faculties, refines the tastes, elevates the feelings, they cannot discern the practical use.[1]

Thus the sway of theology was replaced by that of materialism and pragmatism. The clergy, once respected and influential, had become a caricature for 19th-century novelists. Martineau described

the Episcopalian clergyman, insular and national, steeped to the lips in the academic tincture of Oxford or Cambridge, presumed to be a gentleman without the trouble of proving it, and sure to be the scholar rather than the divine,—the Nonconformist minister, bourgeois in his manners, American in his politics, cosmopolitan in his philanthropy, too little of a Heathen to be a great scholar . . . with a weakness for eloquence, a dependence on popularity, and a contempt for quiet forms of strength.[2]

Martineau added that ministers themselves had become confused about their role, partly because people had such a variety of expectations of them:

He is expected, as pastor, to circulate freely over the vast area from which every Nonconformist Church is gathered; by another, as if he had a parochial charge, to look up the special district of his own chapel, and call the neighbours to his fold; by a third, to go forth as missionary into the villages around, and start fresh centres of kindred life; by a fourth, to work up the schools into the highest efficiency; by a fifth, to be active in the public institutions of the town; by a sixth, to be intellectually in the van of modern knowledge; and by all, to preach always with thought so fresh and heart so deep as to rouse the languid and not disappoint the wise.[3]

All of these expectations so burden the minister that the work is too demanding for any part of it to be done well, said Martineau. The minister, seeking to help the church grow, and wishing to please the congregation, easily loses sight of the primary function of a Christian minister. Sermons are shorter and have less substance, and the liturgy conducted by rote. Instead of striving to impart divine wisdom, ministers pay more attention to the opinions of the leaders of the congregation: "though ordained to declare the whole counsel of God, they have more often studied the taste than the wants of their hearers."[4] Treasures above are compromised in favor of treasures below; ministers seek human praise instead of God's approving voice. Too easily, ministers subdue their consciences with false excuses and decide that they had better keep truth to themselves. But, says Martineau, "every man's own convictions are to him truth, to him are Christianity; and . . . to conceal them is to act the part of the wicked and slothful servant who buried his master's talent in the earth."[5]

Martineau was concerned to restore the reputation of the ministry, and to that end he recommended some institutional changes in the church. For example, he favored the system of paying uniform salaries so that all churches, including the small rural ones, could have well-qualified clergy and sound preaching. He also sought to eliminate what he saw as un-Christian class distinctions so common in the churches.

Martineau also recommended a more rigorous system of training for ministers. He believed that the minister's main task was to bring the people to God, revealed first by the Jewish prophets and patriarchs but more gloriously by Christ.[6] To that end ministers must feel called by God, and churches should examine them on that call when asking them to undertake the charge. Martineau wanted ministers to be selected carefully and trained rigorously, as they were the guardians of the gospel and Christ's representatives in society. He wanted a professional ministry well trained in all areas of church work.

Martineau also had plenty of professional advice for ministers themselves. It was a mistake, he said, for ministers to measure the success of their positions by the size of membership and attendance. He urged them to resist the pull of public opinion—not to preach merely what is popular instead of sticking with the stern demands of the gospel, and to remain firm about opposing popular sins.

For Martineau, the primary function of the church was public worship, and the minister functioned as its leader. Martineau knew that ministers could become so involved with expanding their roles in the community and with congregational needs that they failed to take time for reflection and study on what they were trying to do, how their role as Christian messengers was intended to lead the congregation into a closer relation to God, and how the church became part of the larger Christian endeavor. He wrote about several aspects of leadership in ministry: a learned ministry, the minister's position as ambassador of Christ, and the need for ministers to consider their sacred calling.

Ministers, he said, must feel a sacred calling as servants of God, to preach and pray from the heart. The concept of a call recognizes that the minister is instructed by something more than human. Therefore, instead of bowing to the wishes of the congregation, said Martineau, the minister should remind the people that they are not alone. When he conducted the first communion in the new Manchester College chapel in Oxford, Martineau said, "But here [in the chapel], no one is alone; each is with the little band of first disciples, listening to their Master's parting words, and receiving from his hands, as soon to be stretched forth and pierced, the bread which he brake and the cup which he tendered."[7] A church, said Martineau, is intended to bring the soul into intimate communion with God. Ministers are people among the congregation, not priests set apart. Because they know and share the frailties, sorrows, and aspirations of the people, they can interpret their experiences in sermons and acknowledge them in prayer.

Martineau could speak of sharing the sorrows of the people in part because he knew of the difficulties of the profession from his own experience and from his wide acquaintance with other ministers: "few, perhaps, have any conception how depressing are the anxieties, how overpowering the responsibilities, how intense the mental and moral effort which our duties entail."[8] He also saw how easily worldly success and business claims could interfere with religious virtues. The world demands industry, prudence, and success; and such values as piety, scholarship, and compassion tend to be measured against those qualities: do they achieve success, aid in growth, or produce verifiable results? Roman Catholic clergy, Martineau believed, understood their mainly sacramental role, but the role of the Protestant ministry, especially the Dissenting, was less easily defined.[9]

Yet, if Martineau understood the hardships of the ministry, he was also aware of its rewards. It is a life, he said, given to intellectual pursuits, spiritual development, and service to all that is holy, just, and good. In their work, ministers are stimulated by the expectations of their congregations and must win their approbation. The difficulties in the ministry, Martineau said, come mostly from within, from the minister's lack of clarity about role and responsibilities, rather than from without.[10] Martineau urged ministers to look far ahead, to think about what they want to accomplish in their work, not to be disheartened by temporary setbacks or criticisms, and to remain open to spiritual truth from all sources. He said, "[I] have increasingly dreaded the corroding influence, upon inward love and reverence, of inappreciative criticism of other's beliefs and doctrinal pride in one's own."[11]

If these difficulties can be overcome, the opportunity to serve offers great reward and gratification. Often, however, this requires economic sacrifice. When he resigned Hope Street Church, Liverpool, Martineau wrote his congregation about taking up his duties at Manchester New College, London:

> I must therefore have the sorrow of resigning into your hands next Autumn the office I have so long held, and quitting the service and the scene endeared by a thousand ties. . . .
>
> Gain does not tempt me; for I go to a poorer life;—or Ambition; for I retire to a less conspicuous;—or Ease; for I commit myself to unsparing labour. . . . In the Church of Christ, each has to place his gifts and opportunities at disposal for the divine economy of the whole.[12]

Martineau gave an evaluation of his own ministry when he resigned as minister of Little Portland Street Chapel, London, having served the church for 14 years. In a letter dated February 2, 1873, thanking his congregation for their parting gifts, he wrote:

> In taking leave of a ministry remembered by me chiefly for its aspirations and its regrets, I naturally ask what feature in it can

have elicited this affecting recognition. Shrinking from party action and averse from the zeal of sects, I have been compelled to work in quiet and alone; with no other plan of life than to do the immediate duty as it came, and to plead for each element of Divine truth and goodness exactly as and when it became clear to me, heedless of its bearings on the systems and interests of the day.[13]

2. The Role of the Minister

In Martineau's understanding, the minister's primary role as leader of public worship is to declare the truth and to interpret what God has spread before us through Christ, whose emissaries we are. We, like Christ, are born of nature and born of God: "[W]e too must traverse the desert and meet the fiends of temptation: we have a baptism to be baptized with; and how are we straightened until it be accomplished? We have the path of self-denial to tread, and the midnight watch to meet, and the heavy cross to bear upon the dolorous way; only never alone, for the Father is with us."[14] Ministers, he says, must let inspiration flow through them to the congregation, bringing them to an awareness of themselves as partners with God and recipients of grace.

The true role of the minister, said Martineau, is to serve as an ambassador from God, and the true function of ministry is to increase the influence of Christianity in the world. In the response at his ordination, Martineau laid out his understanding of the roles and duties of ministers: "These, then, I regard as the primary duties of the Christian minister; to awaken devotion to God, obedient faith in our Lord Jesus Christ, and practical expectation of eternity."[15]

Martineau's ministry was Christian in that he followed Christ's teachings about God and sought to follow Christ's example. Christ, thought Martineau, had what we all have within: the voice of God to direct us, if only we will listen. God has many manifestations, but the chief are in the human heart, conscience, mind, and experience. Martineau added that God's will is contained in the Jewish and Christian Scriptures, though he did not say whether he believed Scripture to be the exclusive or the main source of God's will.[16] He said that the minister has a duty to apply critical history and philosophy to understanding the Bible—the one task that sets ministers apart from laypeople.[17] Then Martineau added a point that became especially pronounced in his later ministry: "His most valuable guides are his own mind, and his own conscience; and his most valuable privilege in the use of these, is his unquestionable right of private judgment."[18] The implication was that mind and conscience are to be used toward understanding the Bible. Later Martineau held them to be the primary means of knowing God. For Martineau, the Christian minister is a disciple of Christ and has the duty to ennoble the conscience and inspire reverence and piety in people. The minister helps keep the hearts of the congregation directed toward God through wonder, reverence, and admiration.

Martineau understood that the minister may fill many roles, such as teaching, educating, and urging social action, but he believed these roles should not impinge on the critical task of leading worship. In particular, he believed that instruction as such should be secondary to the task of bringing people to God and should thus remain peripheral to worship. Ministers, he said, may be tempted to include what they have learned of theology, science, history, and biblical criticism in their sermons, but this deflects from the primary purpose of bringing the congregant to God. Such teaching from the pulpit is often self-serving and confusing for the listeners, who find it easy enough to be distracted. Teaching in worship should focus on spiritual development.

Martineau noted that there are three different acceptable ways to teach. First is the ordinary use of the term: to give information. This involves external facts and the use of memory, and it is the method used with children. Duty and faith can be taught partially in this way: teachers provide children with maxims and rules and relate an incident or story to illustrate the point. This teaching by rote, however, does not impart goodness. Said Martineau of one who is taught this way: "he has been broken in like an animal, not converted as a Christian."[19]

A second and superior way of teaching, said Martineau, is the formation of character. This method cultivates the divine nature that God has planted in us, through which we are aware that some activities are admirable and noble, others disgusting. Character must be made strong if it is to withstand the lures of power, fame, and wealth. The third and best way of teaching, said Martineau, is to bring people to understand the moral law, by which every virtue is admired, and only virtue is admired. This moral law is taught by starting with comparative morals, then discussing different types of ethical choice and manners of distinguishing between them.[20]

Martineau believed the teaching role of the minister to be subordinate to the conduct of public worship. Teaching is an adjunct, which is done through lectures, classes, discussions, a variety of forms of publishing, and, of course, by example. Clearly Martineau valued the role of education; he was, after all, a professor and a college principal, whose many published works were designed to educate.

Martineau believed that the minister's pastoral role was also important, subordinate only to the duties of bringing people to God and teaching. Ministers, he said, know grief and sorrows, and they must help people to see beyond them:

> [W]hatever scope there may be, in the great Infirmary of human ills, for faithful labour in every form, some at least there ought ever to be who, while not slow to bind the wounded and tend the cup of cold water, can look beyond the suffering symptoms of the hour, or even the epidemic of the day, and following the maladies of our humanity to their deepest ground can obey the Supreme Physician's voice, "Bring them hither to me."[21]

Ministers are more than counselors. They are the representatives of God who assure people that the bad times they experience are not without some purpose, that they are beloved children of the Father, and that the moral law affirms that, in the end, wrongs are righted and our suffering justified.

3. The Need for a Learned Ministry

The need for a learned ministry was obvious and compelling to Martineau. Ministers, he said, must be able to lead and persuade with carefully reasoned arguments and know how to stir religious impulses in people. During the early Christian era, one might have succeeded by claiming to have mystical experiences of the divine, a special call, or a divine mission, but such times, he said, are no more. The time had gone when the clergy enjoyed advantages and influence simply because of their profession. Ministers, he said, must now be conversant with the trends of the time and be able to present their ideas in the light of modern science, biblical criticism, philosophy, and the events that shape people's thinking. They must be aware of rapid developments in science, industry, politics, and the humanities, as well as changing attitudes and values. Martineau acknowledged the decline, if not the disappearance, of the belief that the pastor is the heir of the apostolic office and speaks with special authority.[22] Authority must now come from education, said Martineau, and churches now need a highly educated ministry, if they are to cope with the needs of society: "The feelings toward the Christian ministry have changed; and the change is such as to demand a more enlightened class of men, in order to make it yield the same results."[23]

Leadership in society, said Martineau, will rest with those who combine intellectual with moral power. Ministers are expected to provide not only guidance for the conduct of church affairs, but also moral guidance in the community. Although he believed he minister should be cautious about interfering in political matters, Martineau himself readily took positions on broad matters of public interest, such as education for the poor, women's rights, the threat of technology, and equal treatment for all religious groups.

The need for such leaders was particularly pressing in the Dissenting ministry, which did not have a strong tradition of ministerial authority or sacramental offices to sway and satisfy the people. Martineau saw his main task as Principal of Manchester College to provide the difficult education and training that was needed:

> The Institution whose work we resume to-day provides for the full Academic training of a permanent succession of Nonconformist Ministers. Its very design, therefore, assumes the perpetual need in Christian society of religious guides and instructors; the natural relation of their work to the whole circle of human knowledge; and the possibility of a Scientific Theology where there is no bespoken conformity. To these principles, and to the high estimate which they imply of the Christian preacher's office, we firmly adhere, in the face of social discouragement and of philosophical disparagement.[24]

Given the changed social situation of his day, Martineau thought ministerial training should be pursued in three stages. First, the prospective minister should obtain an undergraduate degree at a university. Then divinity training should follow. Finally, the District Board should test the minister according to its own requirements.[25] Further, in a speech proposing a national church, he argued that formal training be required for employment: "liberty might be given to parishes, after some regulated compromise with the patrons,—to elect their own ministers,—no one being eligible except a person with a University degree and ordination or recognition according to the usages of some one denomination known to the law."[26] Martineau also felt the importance of continuing one's scholarly pursuits after entering the ministry. The minister, he said, must have a thorough background not only in the classics but in the great thinkers of more recent times. The purpose of reading, though, is not just to find out what prominent people thought, but to stimulate one's own mind. On the importance of reading, Martineau wrote:

> And then how much of the best inward life of all Christians depends upon books. Drain away the sources of a permanent and satisfying literature, cut off from the future its Locke and Lardner, its Taylor and Wellbeloved,[27] its Priestley and Channing, and do you think that, for a religion so starved, there would be any history at all? Take the volumes from its shelves, blot out the dear and venerable names that are the symbols of its wisdom and piety; and what Church could live? They are the

silent preachers that reach the furthest onward, and find the deepest in all time.[28]

At the same time, Martineau was aware of the difficulties presented by a minister's speaking in a language the laity does not understand. He wrote to his friend Richard Hutton on a problem they shared:

> I quite understand, my dear Richard, your mortification at being called too profound in your preaching. You will be happy if the charge does not follow you, as it does me, through life, and repeat itself week by week, till your heart is ready to sink in despair. The passion for what is called plainness seems very strange in people whose religion lies in the gospel of John and the epistles of Paul. I believe that we must bear up against this reproach, and speak faithfully what is given us to say, without much regards to that standard of usage which regulates "intelligibilities."[29]

Although Martineau didn't like this situation, he felt it was inevitable. He thought in long, complex sentences. Not only was his language convoluted but his thoughts often were beyond the comprehension of the average person. Many of his ideas would be understandable if read but they were extremely difficult to understand on one hearing. He was aware that his penchant for such language diminished his influence, but he had to be true to himself.

Although Martineau resisted the impulse to simplify his sermons, he also acknowledged the importance of truly addressing the needs of the congregation. He saw that some congregants suffered because of "wonder disappointed, of conscience unaided, of reverence unexercised, of aspiration sent thirsting away."[30] Such people may suffer great problems in life, and they may have little interest in technical theology, abstract logic, or discoveries in archaeology or biblical criticism. This kind of learned preaching talks down to them; it is "consecrated libel from the lips least entitled to pronounce it,—uttered by some shallow-hearted closet-priest."[31]

Similarly, Martineau, like all those who teach ministerial students, faced the problem of how to balance academic with practical training. He found it hard to balance such disciplines as systematic theology, biblical criticism, philosophy, logic, and church history against administration, organizational work, social action, community participation, pastoral relations, liturgics, and homiletics. This was a problem Martineau never solved satisfactorily, and in fact he himself was not successful in building churches. Little Portland Street barely stayed afloat and did not long outlast his ministry.

Nonetheless, Martineau continued to hold that one can be—indeed, must be—both a good minister to the congregation and a good scholar: "It would be strange indeed if they who are kindled with some few rays of his intellectual light were not also nearer to him in tenderness, in patience, in constancy of beneficent activity."[32] He said further: "If we do not develop the scholarly accomplishments we will speak only to those of lower level and the intellectual development of the churches will become stagnant. The prophet must be a theologian also: and cold as may seem the winds that stir the waters of thought, they are needed to quicken the pulses of the heart, to flush the cheek with love, and brace the will to act."[33] The essential point was that ministerial learning must be in the service of the congregation and its needs.

For Martineau, ministerial training and education assumed a commitment as a Christian minister by one who recognizes discipleship to Jesus Christ. During his own lifetime, Martineau saw increasing reticence among his students about that kind of commitment, yet he remained firm in his belief that it was essential. Regarding an application for the ministry by a man who was a theist but not a Christian, Martineau wrote: "My position is that, if (by Triennial Meeting or otherwise) we are to have an organized Church, identical with that whose chapels and churches we inherit, it must continue to be Christian; else, the identity is lost, and inheritance is forfeited."[34] Thus Martineau believed that education alone is not adequate preparation for the ministry; it must be within the context of a serious commitment, a genuine calling to the ministry.

4. Martineau's Advice to Ministers

Martineau offered advice to ministers on both formal and informal occasions. He gave the Charge to the Minister at numerous inductions, and on many occasions he opened college sessions or delivered the Valedictory at the close of college sessions. He wrote advice in letters, lectures, and addresses, and advice is scattered through some of his books. His views on the learned ministry and the need for a strong sense of commitment have already been noted. Examining the other advice he gave other ministers will also help illuminate his view of the ministry and its role in worship. First, Martineau urged ministers to be natural in the pulpit, not to treat it as a stage or an opportunity to call attention to themselves. Notably, in his own sermons, first-person pronouns are rare. Of self-serving preaching, he wrote: "Leave it, we entreat you, to actors, whose business it is to represent and not to be,—to set their laugh to music, and accentuate the 'crescendo' and 'diminuendo' of their grief: but let the chief of all realities remain a first-hand simplicity."[35] Such simplicity, Martineau believed, would best serve the congregation.

Obviously, ministers should have integrity in and out of the pulpit, but Martineau saw many temptations for them to overcome: the desire for popularity, the wish not to offend, the tendency not to scold because it would damage the self-respect and self-esteem of parishioners. Martineau's answer to these temptations was to look within and obey the voice that tells us to respect what we most revere, not to compromise with what we know is hateful. All of this, he said, is part of doing God's will. When we speak thus we speak the words of the Father, whose servants we are.[36]

Integrity in the ministry also included several other facets. Pretense and insincerity, said Martineau, have no place in the ministry. The minister cannot preach, impart faith to others, or lead worship without a personal understanding of faith. To that end, ministers must also avoid negativism: "When we meet to pray, and find some sanctity for our life, no one has any right to expect a treatise on what we don't think true; and we profane our duty, if, instead of scattering the seed of life, we go about proving that a husk is a husk."37 Thus, said Martineau pretense, insincerity, and negativism weaken the effectiveness of the ministry.

Worship may also become tired and stale, said Martineau, if ministers do not attend to their own spiritual lives. They cannot give to the congregation what they do not have. That is, neglecting personal spirituality leads to being unprepared for worship, to behaving like a showman, speaking and acting shallowly, not from the heart. Usually, ministers do not deliberately neglect the framing of worship, nor do they intend to come into the pulpit badly prepared. Their weakness, says Martineau, is a creeping sloth. Ministers face the temptation of spiritual laziness in the course of their intellectual growth; they might study philosophy, theology, church history, treatises on the Bible, and a variety of disciplines, yet remain personally untouched. Thus the minister may be inclined

> to study a sacred text as coldly as a newspaper advertisement; to follow the steps of Christ even to Gethsemane, and be within hearing of his voice, yet fall asleep and be unable to watch with him one hour; to say you pray, without praying; to teach about the Spirit of God, yet not be in it; to pass through the Sunday hours with a weekday mind; to dwell on the new-birth with unregenerate heart; and expiate on the solemn grounds of the Infinite Love and the eternal Life with untrembling thought, and soul empty of their wonder and their joy.38

Worship, said Martineau, must be led by one dedicated to the service of Christ's religion. Martineau cautioned against professional traps such as intellectual competition, ambition for recognition, the lure of honors and position, wishes for admiration and praise, and pride in accomplishments. The mind must be disciplined, and the goal of serving God must ever be in the forefront. In a sermon titled "The Negative Faith" (the only instance of his using the word "negative" in a title), Martineau said, "Whatever you relinquish, relinquish simply for its error & unworthiness; whatever you change, change not for easier but for nobler & severer terms of life & duty; not for a lower & more worldly, but for a higher & more aspiring piety;—& you may then stand fast, in the quiet love of God, and the wonder of sceptics & the scorn of Pharisees."39

Perhaps Martineau erred in expecting others to live up to the high standards he set for himself. Stern though he was, he did recognize the need to encourage new ministers in their calling, for their efforts could help bring the Kingdom of God closer. He said to students completing their studies in 1883, "Go then with a heart of faith and courage! The field is clear; set a steadfast hand to the plough, and trace the furrows deep and clean; scatter good seed and spare it not; and may the Lord of the harvest make the ingathering glorious!"[40]

Martineau often reminded his colleagues that worship should awaken people to the Christian virtues. It should arouse sympathy in the cold heart; self-esteem in the forlorn; holiness in the cynic; and compassion in the self-centered. Those who spend their energy on worldly and carnal urges abandon the divine life "and can no more reach their altitudes than the paralytic can climb the Alps."[41] The minister, said Martineau, must waken them from their spiritual slumber, for such people suffer a self-inflicted loss of the divine life: "To the spiritually dead, nothing really lives, but only moves with a meaningless automatism."[42] Through sincere and thoughtful worship, ministers lead their congregations to obedience and faith in God as a partner with Christ, while also urging on them the expectation of eternity. In short, he said, the task of ministry is to declare the truth openly, fearlessly, and plainly, with the highest regard for the monitions of one's own mind:

> And, to younger men, I would say that I believe, upon the whole, there is no rule of life for a preacher that is so safe a guide as that: to shrink at altimes [sic] from stating that which is half true—to themselves, I mean—and to shrink from stating what is false to themselves, but never to shrink, for a moment, from stating that of which they have a deep and profound conviction. . . . [I]t is that [veracity] which alone, in the sphere of religious action, is likely to be crowned by the blessing of Providence.[43]

Notes

1. "The Demand of the Present Age," 42–43.
2. *Essays II*, 334.
3. *National Duties*, 451.
4. *Studies*, 490.
5. *Ibid.*
6. Drummond and Upton I, 55.
7. "Communion Address, 1893," 29.
8. "A Letter, Addressed to the Dissenting Congregation of Eustace-Street," 1.
9. "The Demand of the Present Age," 42–51.
10. *Essays IV*, 13.
11. "Proceedings in Connection with the Resignation of The Rev. James Martineau, Christmas, 1872," 17.*ort of Proceedings, 1857*," 3–4.
13. "Proceedings in Connection with the Resignation of The Rev. James Martineau, Christmas, 1872," 17.
14. *Essays IV*, 11–13.
15. Drummond and Upton I, 27.
16. *Ibid.*, 55.
17. "Address at the Ordination of the Rev. James Martineau," 27–28.
18. *Ibid.*, 28.
19. *Hours II*, 322.
20. *Ibid.*, 322–32.
21. *Essays IV*, 91.
22. "Address, On Occasion of Laying the Foundation Stone of a New Church in Hope Street," 437.
23. "The Demand of the Present Age," 41.
24. *Essays IV*, 76–77.
25. "Suggestions on Church Organisation," 18–19.
26. *Essays II*, 193.
27. A curious inclusion, since Charles Wellbeloved wrote no religious books.
28. *Essays IV*, 15
29. Drummond and Upton I, 337
30. *Essays II*, 340.
31. *Ibid.*
32. *National Duties,* 395.
33. *Essays IV*, 547.
34. MS HMC Davis 1:88.
35. *Essays II*, 338–39.
36. *Ibid.*, 490.
37. Carpenter, 195.

38. *National Duties*, 432–33.
39. "The Negative Faith," 13.
40. *National Duties*, 437.
41. *Ibid.*, 435.
42. *Ibid.*, 435.
43. *The Church of the Future*, 4.

Chapter IV:
Martineau's Sources of Authority

Because of the importance of the minister's role as leader of public worship, understanding the source of ministerial authority is an urgent necessity. To what extent does the minister receive authority from tradition, church hierarchy, and such works as the *Book of Common Prayer*? Martineau labored long to answer this question with a synthesis of the major concepts of the Bible and Christian tradition with the moral law and conscience. In Martineau's understanding, faith comes from within and is confirmed by external sources. He held the traditional sources of authority in high regard, but he saw them as subordinate to intuition and conscience.

In his lecture "Five Points of Christian Faith,"[1] Martineau laid out five tenets that are particularly relevant to the question of authority. First, Martineau believed in the moral perceptions of the human being. We have a faculty—the conscience—that enables us to distinguish between right and wrong, to know what our duty is and what we must shun. Our moral perception, he said, causes us to "love and revere whatever is great and excellent in character, to abhor the mean and base . . . ; that Justice, Mercy, and Truth are good and venerable, is no matter of doubtful opinion, in which peradventure an error may be hid." Second, Martineau believed that God is morally perfect, and that we can know God through our own moral faculty and sense of duty. Third, he believed that our own highest desires and noblest sentiments are part of our divine and inspired character, derived from God, not from social custom or consensus. Fourth, he believed that conscience and moral affections are the only ways God may be revealed inwardly; they are the only faculty of our nature capable of furnishing us with the idea and belief of Him, with any perception of his character, and allegiance to his will. . . . [N]ature, life, history, miracle, notwithstanding their most sedulous discipline, would leave us utterly in the dark about religion, except so far as they addressed themselves to our consciousness of what is holy, just, beautiful, and great. . . . [W]hile regarding the human conscience as the only inward revealer of God, we have FAITH in CHRIST as his perfect and transcendent outward revelation. We conceive that Jesus of Nazareth lived and died, not to persuade the Father, not to appease the Father, not to make a sanguinary purchase from the Father, but simply to 'show us the Father'. . . .[2]

Finally, Martineau believed in human immortality as exemplified by "the heavenly life to which Jesus ascended. . . . To assure us of this great truth, it were enough that Jesus assumed and taught it." That is, Jesus represented the height of human spiritual attainment, and we can all attain what he did.

As highly as he valued the individual search for truth, Martineau also thought there must be agreement within a congregation and, preferably, within the movement as a whole, on the source of authority, on the main features of Christian doctrine, and the essentials of the Christian life. There must be acceptance of a common tradition of faith, which in turn must be grounded in history and a common body of devotional literature. Otherwise, said Martineau, we wander aimlessly and flounder about in confusion as to our mission and goal.

The church, said Martineau, is a worshipping community with a history extending back to the time of Jesus. Throughout this history, it has recorded the experiences of saintly people and every temptation and sorrow that can confound us, along with every noble deed and conquest that can inspire us. Such a store of wisdom provides guides for conduct, understanding of duty, and insight into every new emergency. This historical continuity also serves as a source of authority for the ministry and the church. Martineau argued for acknowledging and preserving the historical context of worship, even as we critique it.

Martineau also wrote at length about the ease with which the power of authority may be abused. For example, he noted that the Catholic Church claimed divine authority, yet it had changed doctrines many times, each time asserting that its latest position was true. He offered many detailed illustrations and catalogued dissidents punished and anathematized. For example, he wrote, Pope Vigilius (537–555) initially sided with the monophysites but in 540 pronounced their ideas anathema.[3] At another time, witchcraft was pronounced the work of the Devil, and the clergy was ordered to "emphatically preach to their parishioners that all this ... is put into men's minds not by a divine being, but by an evil spirit; viz., the Devil, who assumes the form of an angel of light."[4] Originally exorcism was part of every baptism, a remnant today being the clause, "I renounce the Devil and all his works." Such notions, said Martineau, debase the church by appealing to ignorance and superstition. Martineau also wrote of the Inquisition:

> Neither scruples of humanity, nor the dawning light of a returning intellectual civilization, disturbed the resolute persistency of the Church in this superstition [its belief in reports of atrocities during the initiation rites of heretics]. Murmurs, indeed, were heard against the intrusion of Papal officers ... but the pope, who could bear down on such constitutional resistance, had no theological contradiction to expect.[5]

Martineau also detailed the successive condemnations and repeals in the cases of Copernicus and Galileo, finding so many changes in official position that "what was heresy once is heresy no more."[6] In sum, said Martineau, the history of Christendom is one of fierce controversies that always ended with the outvoted minority being cut off as a withered branch and the triumphant majority being proclaimed as the only true Church.[7]

Martineau also noted the Church's history of corruption and violence: "That Church has proved its capacity to defy every injustice except its own, to pit every suffering needless to itself, to banish every darkness deeper than the cloister shade.... License has seldom been carried further than by some of the "holy fathers" on the throne of Peter."[8]

Martineau asserted that "the darkest sins of the declining [Roman] empire are paralleled by the revolting crimes of an ascendant Papacy," and he detailed the crimes of the Borgia popes, their nepotism, their dissolute priesthood, their denunciations of Wycliffe, and their "deep-seated moral putrefaction."[9] His detailed knowledge of the churchly abuses in the Middle Ages is also impressive. Medieval church leaders, he wrote, routed heresy and expressed extreme hatred of differing views. They were politically, morally, and financially corrupt. And, said Martineau, these crimes were endemic in the hierarchy and nature of the Church. In fact, such vile behavior had been endemic to both sacred and secular authorities, at all times, in both Pagan and European cultures. What made these intolerant practices worse in the Church, of course, was that the Church claimed that it possessed divine authority and followed the unchangeable teachings of the Holy Ghost.[10] It should be noted that Martineau did not oppose the Catholic Church and in fact fought hard for its civil and religious liberties. He was, however, critical of the ease with which authority combined with power can be abused, and he resented what he perceived as the extravagant claims of authoritarian churches.

Given the ease with which authority is abused and the speed with which power corrupts, as evidenced in his critique of Catholic history, the authority churches can claim is questionable. Unless we are to rely only on ourselves, without any connection to something greater, said Martineau, we must have some authority for our worship and our exploration of our relation to God. The problem with any external authority, however, is its tendency to prevent free, healthy inquiry—at least inquiry that does not end in the predetermined conclusions set forth by that authority. Naturally, institutions want to preserve their power, and challenges to that power are likely to be regarded as heretical.

Worship is usually validated by the authority of a sacred text, a special revelation, an authority figure, a church hierarchy, or some combination of these. When such things are not used as the final authority for worship, then what source remains? Martineau dealt with that question in many of his writings, sermons, and addresses. His answer was complex and will be discussed here in detail. Martineau's final authority was conscience, which he considered to be the voice of God speaking within us.

He found supporting evidence for this position in reason, the Bible, Christian tradition, the person of Jesus, and the moral law. We will examine each of these sources in turn and the ways Martineau used them to support his concepts of worship and authority.

1. Reason
A. The Supremacy of Reason

Martineau's theology is indebted to Kant, who held that the existence of God could not be proved or disproved, but may be postulated. In his *Critique of Practical Reason*, Kant combined this postulate with morality to argue that that there must be a final reckoning achievable by moral striving, in the next world, if not in this—an argument that appealed to Martineau. Using Kant's ideas of universality, rationality, and impartiality, Martineau developed his belief that the moral law is derived from God and is binding on human will. If we have the duty to do right, he reasoned, there must be a right to be done. In Kant's concept of Absolute Idealism, the ultimate nature of reality is mind or idea, absolute and unchanging. The universe, or nature, is that Absolute expressing itself. Humans, said Kant, are partial manifestations of that idea and our minds are part of the Absolute Mind. Among the moral implications he drew from this philosophy is the concept of the categorical imperative. Martineau translated Kant's philosophical concept of the Absolute Idea (or Absolute Mind) into theological terms, which influenced Transcendentalism in America.

Martineau also participated in the Romantic movement, which stressed inwardness as the way to understand reality: God, he believed, is revealed inwardly. Romanticism was especially amenable to religion and Christianity, because the values of Christianity were grounded in both experience and the historical Jesus. Romanticism dealt, as did Idealism, with the power of the mind. Human life, said the Romantics, is grounded both in observation and experience and in the mind's interpretation of its perceptions. Martineau thought of Jesus as an embodiment or incarnation of the Absolute Idea. Indeed, he said, we all are such incarnations, and Jesus is an exemplar to us of what power resides within the soul or Mind.

Yet Martineau, especially early in his career, also embraced the Enlightenment-era ideas that human reason could penetrate the mysteries of the world, and that happiness could be attained through perfection of the rational life. In his early work *The Rationale of Religious Enquiry, or The Question Stated of Reason, The Bible, and the Church; In Six Lectures* (1836), Martineau challenged the prevailing Unitarian assumption that everything plainly taught in the New Testament, and everything that reasonably could be inferred from it, should be believed. The book, which appeared in four editions over 17 years, did much to establish his reputation.[11] His thesis was that all research into religious truth must have as the final court of appeal the judgment of the human mind: "Neither the first principle, then, of the German Rationalists that reason must judge of the contents as well as the outward structure of revelation; nor their secondary rule that the resources of natural causation must be exhausted before recourse is had to the preternatural, in the explanation of historical phenomena, can be proved unsound."[12]

In *The Rationale*, Martineau argued that no conviction can claim higher authority than the rational. No external authority, not even Scripture, can be higher than the authority of reason, nor can any inspiration establish anything contrary to reason. After all, it is by reason that Scripture is interpreted: "No apparent inspiration whatever can establish anything contrary to reason. . . . [R]eason is the ultimate appeal, the supreme tribunal, to the test of which even Scripture must be brought."[13] Martineau's purpose in The Rationale is to countermand a position dominant among the Unitarians:

> The [Unitarians] have repeatedly said, if we could find the doctrines of the Trinity and the Atonement, and everlasting torments in the Scriptures, we should believe them; we reject them, not because we deem them unreasonable, but because we perceive them to be unscriptural. For my part, I confess myself unable to adopt this language. Not that I entertain any hesitation in pronouncing these notions, in the form in which they now exist, to be unscriptural, or doubt the importance of relieving the Christian records of all responsibility for them. But I am prepared to maintain, that if they were in the Bible,

they would still be incredible; that the intrinsic evidence against a doctrine may be such as to baffle all the powers of external proof.[14]

Later in life, Martineau partially retracted his claim that reason was the ultimate authority, describing *The Rationale* as "a juvenile production which I have long ceased to reproduce."[15] However, that does not mean that he abandoned reason. Martineau continued to insist that the means of discrimination are reason and conscience, "the living organs for the apprehension of truth and holiness."[16]

In part Martineau drew back from his extreme reliance on reason because it, too, could be abused, and because it gave too much power to those who would undermine religion. As he said in a sermon, "There is something strange and unintelligible in the anxiety of a pretended rationalism to get rid of the inspiring God, to make sure that our nature will be quite let alone, to environ it with an impassable ring-fence, and plant sentry-boxes of argument all round, to exclude the possible encroachments of anything Divine."[17]

B. The Limits of Reason

Reason is to be used wisely, said Martineau, and to turn against it is a grave error because it is the means of testing the truth of any proposition. Arguing that reason should not be cowed by the force of authority, he wrote: "To appeal to my reason, and then, if I cannot see the force of the proof, to hold me up as a blasphemer and a rebel against the word of God, is an inconsistency, of which only the degenerate followers of the great Apostle [the Pope] could be guilty."[18]

Martineau firmly believed reason could contribute to the search after the holy: why should not the prophet and the philosopher be one and the same? There should be no conflict, he said, in joining intellect and will with adoration. Martineau was disturbed by the common habit of belief without rational grounds, with reference to an outside authority alone. When the Rev. Dr. Allon, President of the Congregational Union of England and Wales, criticized his 1881 speech "Loss and Gain in Recent

Theology," Martineau replied,

> [Dr. Allon] believes in the Incarnation. On what evidence? The introductory chapters of Matthew and Luke? Even were they not hopelessly at variance with each other, would even a credulous historical critic accept such a narrative on such testimony, were it the prefix to any religion other than his own? . . . In treating . . . as true and right what, from any other source, the reason and conscience would not receive as such, I do not see that I am open to correction.[19]

Martineau believed that reason must not be contradicted by belief. Yet, he acknowledged later in life, reason is not the final authority. Reason is properly a critical tool, but it is not religion itself. We err, he said, when we believe only what can be demonstrated by reason. Martineau was philosopher enough to know that "proof" is a term of logic requiring premises that are not subject to proof. Reason is a servant, not a master, and, used alone, it may destroy belief. Such an error, wrote Martineau, is

> to introduce into the gospel that fatal canker which, in the ancient world, enfeebled and dissolved system after system, and left the most splendid remains of speculative genius and ethical wisdom on a social soil dark with unpitied miseries and festering with moral corruptions. Who does not know, out of his own heart, that he never was reasoned into holy wonder, love, or reverence? And who can fail to observe, that there is no fixed proportion between force of understanding and clearness or depth of religion?[20]

In sum, said Martineau, reason can assist belief, but it cannot produce faith. Faith comes from "communion together upon holy things; and by trustful surrender to which we may become one in Christ."[21] The trouble with reason is that we tend to exalt it, which may lead us to deny God in the absence of physical, sensory evidence: "Nothing more arbitrary, nothing narrower, can well be conceived than to lay down the rule, that our lowest endowment,—the Perceptive powers which introduce us to material things,—have the monopoly of knowledge; and that the surmises of the Moral sense have nothing true, and the vaticinations of devoted Love only a light that leads astray."[22] The senses are to be trusted, Martineau explains, but we also have other faculties: imagination shows us beauty; the spirit induces the spiritual in us; the moral law appeals to our conscience and will. Thus reason is an aid to, but not a replacement for, spiritual insight.

Thus, for Martineau, reason is an important source of authority, which helped to replace the earlier authority of the Bible. Yet, as we have seen, shortly after publication of *The Rationale of Religious Inquiry*, reason began to take a subordinate place in Martineau's conception of authority. Likewise, the Bible still retained an important place in his thought.

2. The Bible
A. The Older Belief

Unitarian worship in Martineau's time relied, as it had for many years, on biblical authority, and sermons were expected to be expositions of a text that illustrated the application of doctrine to life. The Bible was the primary authority in most of the Protestant world, having replaced the hierarchical authority of the Catholic and other churches. It was the main authority in Unitarianism, too; the Unitarians of Martineau's day rejected such doctrines as the Trinity, human depravity, the deity of Christ, and the vicarious atonement solely on the grounds that those doctrines neither appeared in Scripture nor could reasonably be inferred from it. Unitarians claimed that they would adopt any of the above doctrines if they could be shown to derive from Scripture. Most Christians of Martineau's day believed that the authors of the New Testament were fully inspired throughout, like secretaries taking down what was dictated to them by the Holy Spirit.

Inherent in the Unitarian position, however, was the problem of how the different accounts of the Synoptic Gospels were to be reconciled. If external authority was rejected as the arbiter of such difficulties in interpretation, then what other authority could be substituted? Influenced by the new science of the higher criticism, the Unitarians used debate, argumentation, and reason to interpret the meaning of disputed parts of the gospels and epistles and to reconcile the many variations—which led them into controversial positions that they were slow to acknowledge to themselves. They sought to keep their dissent quiet, without attracting undue notice. After all, Unitarianism had been a criminal offense in England until 1844.[23] Even in Martineau's day Unitarians continued to suffer some forms of legal persecution; for example, they were denied matriculation into the universities until 1871.

Most Unitarians wanted to be accepted as part of the mainstream of Christianity, at least among Dissenters, and the occasional radical was an embarrassment to them. If the Bible is taken to be something other than divine revelation, they asked, what then might follow? They had rejected one orthodox doctrine after another. Might they also repudiate resurrection, the centrality of Christ, and so much of the Christian tradition that sanctioned the values cherished by society? Could they then even claim the title Christian? What would happen to morals?

Thus Unitarians had reasons for not wanting to muddy the waters unduly. The majority of Unitarians held to the authority of the Bible. But Martineau was different. He said in an 1835 address:

> The tendency among us (a tendency not, I think, likely to be arrested) is toward the belief that the Sacred Writings are perfectly human in their origin, though recording superhuman events; that the Epistles abound in the discussions of questions now obsolete; that the Gospels, with one exception [John], were constructed from earlier documents, whose origin it is impossible to trace.[24]

Yet Martineau was not just a dabbler in radicalism; he was a thinker with impressive credentials. He used with great effect the developments in the new field of biblical criticism, and, as previously noted, he was also learned in the sciences and other disciplines. The 1836 publication of *The Rationale of Religious Inquiry* did much to wean Unitarians from reliance on the Bible as their authority. Martineau later retracted some of the stronger stands that he had pronounced in *The Rationale*, but he always argued against the importance of the Bible as the highest authority.

In Martineau's view, religion progressed through the gradual weakening of external authority, whether hierarchical or biblical. When the

Protestants broke from the Catholic Church, he explained, the authority ("the yoke," he called it) of the Church was replaced with the authority of the Bible. Then that too was overthrown: in his own day, the notions that "'the Bible, and the Bible only, is the religion of Protestants,'—that 'Scripture is the Rule of faith and practice,'—are indeed full of historical interest, but for minds at once sincere and exact, have lost their magic power."[25] It was inevitable, said Martineau: remove one authority, and the next one becomes suspect. Thus the standing of the Bible as a divine statute-book was now a relic of a bygone age: "The time is past," he said, "when a doctrine could save itself from criticism by taking refuge under an apostle's word, or a futurity authenticate itself by a prophet's forecast, or a habit become obligatory by evangelical example."[26]

These views are truisms for Unitarians today, but 19th-century Unitarianism was slow to embrace them. His views were shared by Channing and Emerson, but they had more immediate influence in America than he had in England. Martineau's influence was felt most strongly only after his death.

B. Biblical Criticism

The change in Unitarian attitudes toward the Bible did not result from radical or anarchic philosophy, but from critical investigation. "Within the last fifty or sixty years," Martineau wrote in 1881, "we have discovered . . . that the Bible is not susceptible of this kind of use [as] a Divine Text-book."[27] No magic was required to understand one critical point: the infallible inspiration that had been claimed for the Bible was nowhere claimed in the Bible itself.[28]

Martineau devoted a full sermon to tracing the research in biblical history and criticism over a century.[29] This research, he explained, had shown that the Bible was not historically accurate and had disproved one after another of the beliefs that had shored up the authority of the Bible. He also spoke of developments in Old and New Testament criticism, both higher and lower. Rigorous examination using the new critical methods, explained Martineau, had destroyed any rational basis for literal belief in the supernatural events depicted in the Bible. In their efforts to demonstrate the moral beauty of Christianity, the authors of the Bible added elements that, in our modern understanding, strain credulity. We cannot believe in the literal truth of the miracles, for example, with only anonymous testimony to support them.

It should be noted that Martineau was a moderate in this area. He did not agree with the rationalist school of German theology, which had arisen out of the debates on biblical criticism. That school, said Martineau, focused too much on finding areas of agreement instead of exploring challenging points of disagreement: "in short . . . to save the ark of God by throwing over the masts & alas! the rudder to the storm. . . ."[30] Martineau rejected the wholesale overthrow of all that the Bible had been understood to be. On the other hand, he believed he had to address the development of biblical criticism, so that it could be used to aid in our understanding of the will of God through the life and message of Christ.

If both the earlier authoritarian attitude and the excesses of the German rationalists were to be rejected, however, Martineau had to offer new criteria by which to judge the Bible. We have many resources, Martineau said: the natural sciences, the appeal to conscience, and the development of history. We must change our focus, moving away from inquiry on the origins of the Bible toward attempts to understand the inherent truths of the Bible's teachings. Each idea in Scripture must be examined by the means appropriate to that specific teaching. The Logos, for example, should be examined by speculative metaphysics. Other parts or doctrines should be measured by methods such as historical investigation, philosophical research, and inquiry into the intellectual, moral, and spiritual faculties of humanity so as to achieve what harmony they could among the different ideas and doctrines in the Bible.[31]

C. Against Biblical Literalism

Martineau believed that the New Testament books had been written by human beings, in completely human ways, though they record superhuman events. Those who wrote the New Testament, he said, were good and able authors who relied on their memory and reasoned from their own intellects. Further, their impressions were subject to the vagaries of their own imaginations and colored by their own cultural and educational backgrounds. They wrote with devotion and honesty, he said, but within a flawed framework.

The majority of English people in Martineau's day believed the Bible to be literally true, but Martineau believed that that was changing. Too much credulity was now required to believe the literalist position: "We are not averse to the supposition that Moses might be neither geologist nor astronomer; the Tower of Babel does not stand in the way of researches into origin of languages; the age of Methuselah is no longer a vital point. . . .'[32]

The changing understanding of the Bible as authority posed an added difficulty for preachers. When the Bible was considered fully inspired, with every part infallible, they could more easily apply its messages to the problems of the congregation. For any question that arose, one could appeal to the Bible. Now, Martineau understood, the task was harder. Human authorship of the Bible, whether or not of supernatural events, could be the result of misunderstanding; the Epistles discussed questions now obsolete; and the Gospels were based on earlier documents, whose origins could not be traced and whose fidelity could not be tested sufficiently against external sources. Martineau believed the trend toward the humanization of the Bible would continue with the further development of biblical criticism, the discovery of more documents, and further understanding of ancient history and languages.

That change also had consequences for religious education. Martineau argued that the Bible should be taught not as the full will and testament of God, but as containing the spirit of Christ. It must be studied, he said, to see what it tells of duty and hope, but he warned, "This indiscriminate use of the Bible, as an infallible whole, fills the mind with a system of confused and self-contradictory ideas, both of religion and of morals."[33]

But how can one decide which parts of the Bible are true? How does the belief that the Bible is a fallible, human work help to establish guides in worship? These were difficult questions, but Martineau saw his method as the correct one. The Bible, he said, simply has errors and contradictions. For example, it contains teachings that are no longer valid, and its understanding of science is inadequate for our day.

Likewise, plenary inspiration of the Scriptures simply was out of the question for Martineau: "I believe St. Matthew to have been inspired; but I do not believe him to have been infallible. I am sure that he nowhere puts forth any such claim: and if he does not affirm it himself, I know not who can affirm it for him."[34] Martineau pointed out numerous variations and inconsistencies in the gospels,[35] and he scorned the idea that faith requires us to accept them all as equally true. The factual basis of the New Testament episodes need not affect faith. It is far better for our faith to move past such considerations and proceed to the moral and spiritual messages:

> [S]uppose that the first three Gospels are shown to be not personally authentic, not the independent productions of three apostolic men; but a compilation of very composite structure, consisting of (we will say) some thirty fragments, obviously from different hands, and all of anonymous origin. In such case, the individual testimony of eye-witnesses being gone, the whole edifice of external proof which supports a dogmatic Christianity, must fall. But the self-evidence of an oral and spiritual Christianity, of a Christianity that clings to the person and spirit of Christ, is not only unharmed, but even incalculably increased.[36]

The Bible, said Martineau, "neither is, nor pretends to be, a creed and code: We have therefore no Authoritative Text-book of Divine Truth and human Duty: So we must open our minds to all that speaks divinely to them, whether in the Bible or elsewhere."[37] In short, said Martineau, the Bible is to be used in worship as a guide, not a rule. The Bible is not an oracle, and its writings cannot be taken as definitive or conclusive authorities. Its contents are inconsistent and confusing; they depend on too many varying manuscripts; they contain many obscure words with unknown meanings; and the books are often at odds both within themselves and between one another. The Bible, said Martineau, is valuable because of its spirit, not its letter.

D. The Importance of the Bible

The Bible, said Martineau, gives us permanent guides for the spirit. Its moral principles can shed light on our own needs and situations when we understand its history and background, and it belongs to all people of all times:

> Religion is reproached with not being progressive: it makes amends by being imperishable. The enduring element in our humanity is not in the doctrines which we consciously elaborate, but in the faiths which unconsciously dispose of us, and never slumber but to wake again. What treatise on sin, what philosophy of retribution, is as fresh as the fifty-first Psalm? What scientific theory has lasted like the Lord's Prayer?[38]

Martineau claimed that he valued the Bible more, not less, because of his acceptance of critical research on the Scriptures. Are we the poorer, he asked, because we view the Bible as human literature instead of a Divine textbook? Instead of despairing, he wrote: "I claim it as a noble though severe advantage that we are driven from words to realities, and must sink right home to the inward springs of religion in our nature and experience."[39] When the Bible was taken as the literal work of God, it was beyond criticism, thus giving up the real power it could have as a struggle by people to know God's will. "The Bible," he said, "is the great autobiography of human nature, from its infancy to its perfection."[40] It is the agony of humanity writ large. We may put aside the historical parts, said Martineau; even if the stories of Jesus' birth were true (for he felt both could not be), what difference would that make? In the miraculous stories of healing, he said, whether those people were healed is a matter of historical speculation, and belief in them must not be a test of our faith. But when miracles are put aside we go to the heart of the matter: the Bible conveys the gift of God to our comprehension through Christ.

The Bible tells us about Christ, in Martineau's words "a Being so unimaginable, except by the great Inventor of beauty and Architect of nature himself, that I embrace him at once, as having all the reality of man and the divinest inspiration of God."[41] We are attracted to Christ, said

Martineau, because he shows us what we truly are; so compelling is he that in our contemplation of his nature our souls are transformed. The Bible is an important source of our faith and morals, and it provides the conscience with historical and theological context. It contains wisdom that is relevant to eternity, not temporary life. Too easily, Martineau said, we engage in ordinary commerce and industry, wrapped up in our momentary cares, and become distracted from the goal of life, which ought to be concerned with immortality and our divine nature. Some critics complain that the Bible does not deal with the pressing issues of daily life, and Martineau agreed that was so, but he argued that in fact we need to be reminded that these temporary concerns are not the great problems. Thus, as we have seen, Martineau examined reason and the Bible as sources of authority and, on reflection, found them insufficient. Although he valued both reason and the Bible, they no longer seemed to provide the final authority he wanted. He then turned to the examination of another commonly accepted source of authority, tradition.

3. Tradition

Tradition after the Apostolic age was not an important source of authority to Martineau. He rejected creeds and confessions of faith because they were human devices that went beyond anything Jesus himself represented, and because they were exclusive. We have no right to demand more than Jesus did, or to be more restrictive than he was, said Martineau; any exclusive form of Christianity would make the disciples more fastidious than the Master. Although Martineau did not believe in the literal veracity of the Bible, he still believed that we can know what Jesus demanded of us. The gospels reveal the character of Jesus, despite variations in details of the accounts of what he said or did. Thus, said Martineau, we may follow the spirit of Jesus, which is what Jesus himself would want. Martineau cited the gospel account of a Jew who came to Jesus and asked what he must do to obtain everlasting life. Jesus did not lay down new rules or conditions; he simply referred to the "old law" written on tablets of stone and in the human heart.[42]

A. Christ as Authority

Those who appeal to tradition trace their ideas back to Jesus, and so Martineau began there too. Martineau wanted a Christianity that derived from its origin in Christ, rather than from secondary sources. Authority for Christianity, he said, must center in the person of Christ even more than in his teachings. Further, he said, defining Christianity in terms of the intellectual structure erected about the nature of Christ has produced much mischief. The power of Christ is immortal, said Martineau, and the true spirit of Christianity is imperishable. This true spirit will emerge as supreme through a concerted, determined effort to understand it. Indulging a good-natured tolerance or indifference is not enough: "There is no short cut, no lazy path, to a true Christian love."[43] It is tempting to focus on the accounts of what Jesus said or did, but they do not lead us to a real understanding of Jesus. It is his character that instructs us. This is a more difficult path to understanding, said Martineau, but the best one. Martineau had a sentimental and affectionate view of Jesus:

> The story of Jesus, the submissive child, the meek & holy prophet, the friend of the friendless, the guiltless soother of the guilty, the compassionate restorer from the grave, the indignant denouncer of hypocrisy in power & the preacher of glad tidings to the poor; the crucified & yet triumphant, the mortal clothed with immortality;—this touching tale can never cease to find a place in hospitable hearts, &, by transfusion of reverence into human affections, convert them into divine. It is thus in fact that Christianity has lived through the past.[44]

Thus Jesus, as human, instructs us because we have the same potential he had. Yet if he is not God in the orthodox sense, then whence derives his authority?

Christ's authority, Martineau said, comes primarily from his intimacy with God. Martineau believed Jesus was not unique in his receptivity to God, but differed from others in the degree of his reception and commitment. Jesus instructs us about our own divinity: we look at Jesus and see what we might become. Thus Martineau wrote:

> Jesus has given us a fresh faith never held before, and still too much obscured, in the affectionateness of the Great ruler; has made Him our own domestic God, whose ample home encircles all, leaving not the solitary, the sinner, or the sad without a place in the mansions of his house; has wrapped us in the Divine immensity without fear, and bid us claim the warm sun in heaven as our Paternal hearth, and the vault of the pure sky as our protecting roof.[45]

In numerous sermons, Martineau elaborated his ideas of God and how they derived from his understanding of Christ. "It is past all dispute," he said, "that the class of feelings which Jesus enjoined in the first commandment are those of moral veneration. . . . [H]e would inspire us with that love of God which is the love of perfect excellence; it is as the Original of all moral distinctions. . . . "[46] Continuing, he spoke of Christ as "the Revealer of the idea of duty, and the ineffable sanctities of conscience; as the inventor of the humanities of life; as the archetype of whatever is beautiful and noble and tender. . . . [I]t is in such characters as these which exhibit the moral nature of the Infinite Spirit, that we are called on to render him the love of our whole minds."[47]

Martineau did not rely on Christian history for any authority, not even the history of Christ himself. The only point he conceded was that, to be a Christian, one must recognize Christ's historical existence: "All the rest consists in the estimate of his influence, & the reverential appreciation of his mind; which are not acts of a simple judgment, but of the whole spiritual nature."[48]

B. Is Christianity the Superior Way?

In his examination of the Christian tradition, Martineau struggled with the relation of Christianity to non-Christian religions. Early in his career, he believed Christianity to be a superior religion, but he modified his views over the years. If Christianity means following the religion that Jesus advocated, he asked, then why is it superior? Is it just one of many religions of the world? If so, how does it deserve our commitment? Jesus was a Jew; how did he rise above Judaism? The parable of the Good

Samaritan was an example of how a non-Christian might be better than a Christian. Yet Martineau maintained for much of his life that "[t]he Christian religion then, looked at as a realized spiritual fact, the nearest and best known, and, provisionally at least, the highest in the world, occupies, not only justly but inevitably, the centre and main portion of the field."[49]

Later in life, Martineau began to question this basic premise of the superiority of Christianity. He once related an interesting episode, in which he received a letter from an unnamed clergyman. This man wrote that he was a Calvinist and, as such, held that belief in the Incarnation was necessary to be saved and to be considered as a child of God. But, said the cleric,

> I confess that the enormous difficulty of at least apparent facts staggers me; one of the most perfect characters I know is an aged Unitarian lady; but then are there not most exemplary people to be found who deny all Christianity in every shape and form? The more I think of it the more perplexed I am. I should welcome a Revelation from heaven to tell me that I might acknowledge as a child of God anyone who seems to love Him, and his brother, believe or disbelieve what he might.[50]

Martineau responded that blindness to the virtues of one who has a different faith had been branded by Christ himself as hypocrisy:

> To withhold our veneration from goodness because it is not conformed to our own type, or derived from our favourite notions, to sneer at religion which gives forth good fruits,— which touches the conscience, and inspires the affections, and strengthens the will, of its possessors, because we discern an error in its logic, betrays a narrowness of heart . . . entirely at variance with the generous mind of Christ.[51]

A further example to Martineau was the good life of the Hindu Keshub Chunder Sen of India. Upon learning of that man, Martineau said that few under a Christian preacher had ever been moved to such a sense of Christian conviction and Christian humility. He asked, "If Christ had been living now, would he have repelled this Hindoo [sic] when he approached his person? On the contrary, we cannot but admit that here was a soul most congenial to the soul of Jesus; a kind of second John."[52] According to Martineau, the essence of Christianity does not lie in opinions about the person of Christ, but rather in affinity with his spirit and with allegiance to the Divine law that he exemplified. Martineau rejected a faith focused on doctrines about where Christ was before he was born and where he went after he left this life:

> It appears to me that the visit of Chunder Sen was a moral demonstration that our churches are wrong in their definition of Christianity . . . ;—that the essence of it lies not in the doctrinal and historical machinery which envelopes it, but in the spiritual characteristics of which this machinery is the mere vehicle to our souls; that between two men, equally and similarly faithful and devout, the one immediately from personal relation to God, the other mediately through the influence of Jesus Christ, there is no separating difference. . . .[53]

However, noted Martineau, such reasoning may define "Christianity" too broadly. Including non-Christians weakens the meaning of the term "Christian." If it is to include everyone who lives a righteous life, then ethics is substituted for theology, a position Martineau rejected. And if following the will of God is sufficient, then Christ has no centrality. Martineau was entirely honest in his confusion as he faced the dilemma and sought for some rationale for the superiority of Christianity.

Martineau compared Christianity to Judaism and found important distinctions. Judaism, he wrote, is a national religion concentrated in the kingdom of Israel, while Christianity is universal, open to the entire world. "Christianity," he said, "is Judaism bursting all its bounds, flinging away its exclusions and negations, substituting the human race in the place of Israel, and bringing all into divine relations."[54] Christianity is superior to Judaism, said Martineau, because it emerged from the religion of law, which stresses obedience, into the religion of salvation, which stresses gratitude to a deliverer, "and we are capable only of a religion of Reverence, which bows before the authority of Goodness."[55]

In the end, Martineau resolved the central question of the relationship of Christianity to non-Christian religions by asserting that other faiths may be valid for others, but Christianity was most compelling to him: "If there be any who can waft their souls to God on Vedic hymns, or toil upwards by the steps of Gentile metaphysics, far be it from me to question the efficacy of the exercise; it may possibly be as good for them as singing the Athanasian creed. But for myself, both conviction and feeling keep me close to the poetry and piety of Christendom."[56] Martineau saw Christianity as the highest, and therefore for Christians the only revelation, but still believed we should "regard with serious respect, as divinely given to other souls, all earnest faiths that occupy a lower region. . . . Christianity is not so poor a thing that it must put out all other lights before itself can shine."[57] In the end, Martineau's belief in the superiority of Christianity rested on faith in its precepts and their benefits for the human soul. The more we reflect on what Christianity does for the soul, he said, "the less shall we be satisfied with any of the schemes of theology, in or out of Scripture, which undertake to define what it is."[58]

In conclusion, Martineau examined the accepted sources of authority, the Bible and tradition, and his own early conviction that reason would provide the answers he sought. But eventually he judged that all three sources of authority were inadequate. Thus he had to find some other source of authority. Religion consists in duty and responsibility, so he looked to the moral law.

4. The Moral Law
A. The Moral Law and Its Consequences

Worship is predicated on an understanding of what God requires, and Martineau believed that God's will is expressed through the moral law. The obligations we inherit as humans are not arbitrary, nor are they matters of opinion. We do not invent the physical laws of chemistry or physics; we discover them. They exist whether we know them or not, and they are not affected by our attitude toward them. We can ignore or defy these physical laws, but not with impunity. If we abuse the body, seek to defy gravity, or ingest poison, we will suffer the penalty. Likewise, said

Martineau, the universe has inherent moral laws. We do not invent them; rather, as with physical laws, we discover them. They are harder to discern, perhaps, but they exist and can be known through intuition, or direct insight from God, through examining the lessons of history, and through the teachings of inspired people. Religion without the moral law, said Martineau, would not provide a sufficient imperative to duty and responsibility. An understanding of the moral law is also essential to creating positive social change: one cannot achieve a good society without some vision of what good is to be accomplished.

From the premise that there is a moral law that implies duty, Martineau reasoned that acts must have consequences or effects in morals, just as they do in physics. These effects then cause further effects, and a complex chain of reactions ensues. The orderly nature of morality would be violated, just as with physics, if some causes had effects and others did not, or if the effects were erratic and unpredictable, or if the consequences depended on the whim or opinion of the perpetrator. That is, said Martineau, right and wrong is built into the very structure of the universe.

On that much the Unitarians and mainstream Christians generally agreed. But Martineau disagreed with the Unitarians in that he considered punishment, in the future or the hereafter, to be an important part of the moral law. If you put your finger into an electrical socket, you immediately receive a shock. The moral law does not respond so quickly, but it does respond eventually. According to Martineau, either we are free from all obligations or we must be punished for violations of our duty, or sins. "Consistency," he said, "may assail either of these doctrines, but only folly can deny both."[59]

Martineau was stern in his insistence that we accept responsibility for our acts. It is part of our nature, he said, to feel sorry for delinquents and to take note of the social and economic forces that tempted them, but in fact they must take responsibility for their deeds: "if your commiseration be just, the demands of law were cruel & misplaced."[60] Further, he said, "The doctrine of retribution being a solemn truth, appears with all its native force in the teachings of Christ, and arms many of his appeals with a persuasion just and terrible."[61]

Further, Martineau believed that the consequences of human action extended into the life to come. For people to act morally, he wrote, they must believe in immortality. But if a particular belief could assure immortality,

> Must not he who has an entail in the inheritance hereafter, be tempted to become a spendthrift in morals here? ... If a malignant being were to desire a scheme for the demoralization of men, it would appear difficult to devise a surer method than to persuade them that eternal happiness awaited them on conditions perfectly independent of their will; that no act of theirs could either secure or forfeit it.[62]

God judges us by how we are, said Martineau, not by what we believe or how we once were. Martineau did not see God primarily as benevolent, but as just. In this, he disagreed with most Unitarians, who thought of God as a kindly father figure, and with the Universalists, who believed that everyone would be saved. Although Martineau did not believe in eternal punishment, he did believe that our conscience will punish us after death until we reform ourselves. God, said Martineau, is "terrible to all who are inwardly unholy; but not to those who have nothing which they would hide, if they could, from the Searcher of hearts."[63] Thus Martineau posited the source of religious authority in a combination of the external moral law and our internal character.

To Martineau, it made no sense to believe a law of Righteousness is put into our hearts but leads nowhere, with no notice taken of our devotion to it. God has placed a trust in us, but "a trust without a reckoning is a contradiction and a mockery; and as the reckoning most assuredly is not fulfilled in this life, it remains in reserve for ulterior and harmonizing scenes in the drama of our being."[64] Conscience, said Martineau, is placed in us as the voice of God. The conscience persuades us of the moral law; but "a moral world cannot be final, unless it be everlasting."[65]

B. The Moral Law as Intuition

Worship, said Martineau, attempts to bring us into harmony with the highest in the universe. Although worship involves more than morals and ethics, one of its goals is to point the way toward righteous living. The moral law requires us to assume individual responsibility for our own actions; accordingly, evil must be seen as originating from within us, not from without: "To look for a remoter cause than our own guilty wills;—to contemplate it as a Providential instrument, whether we trace it to Adam, to Satan, or directly to God, bewilders the simple perceptions of conscience, and throws doubt on its distinct and solemn judgments."[66] Any theory, Martineau said, that provides us with excuses for our moral lapses, that tells us extraneous forces participate in our guilt, weakens our sense of responsibility.

One consequence of Martineau's belief that the moral law demanded individual accountability was his rejection of the doctrine of the vicarious atonement. God, in Martineau's view, insists that people must pay their own bills: "There are no terms in God's universe on which the selfish can be saved; no;—not if a thousand Calvaries were to repeat to him the divine tragedy of the world."[67] Ethics, always a great concern of Martineau, requires that we understand what is right and that we accept the reasonably foreseeable consequences of our actions. Martineau believed that it would not do to have someone else pay our penalty—that having Jesus pay for our sins was a clear violation of morality.

Martineau wrote extensively on the difficult and complex problem of how one knows the right course of action. Sorting out the correct ethical act, he acknowledged, can be difficult when desires and feelings clash with each other. We may easily find excuses for preferring one path of action to another. To help with this problem, Martineau proposed a rule of relative obligation that took utility into account. "Every action is right," Martineau said, "which, in presence of a lower principle, follows a higher: every action is wrong, which, in presence of a higher principle, follows a lower."[68]

How, then, does one recognize higher and lower principles? Our understanding of moral distinctions, said Martineau, produces in us a noble sense of right and wrong. It is seated in our deepest faculty of reason—an important aid to the conscience, since we can all too easily delude ourselves about our motives and deeds. Reason, said Martineau, is not a substitute for conscience, but it can protect us from the worst abuses. There is a human consensus on which acts are moral, which immoral, said Martineau—an understanding that is not the result of particular individual experiences, for it is no different among different people.

In fact, said Martineau, the sense of the moral law is innate within the conscience, which is God's voice; thus it cannot be taught and is not dependent on education, intellect, or social circumstances: "The difference between good and evil we cannot conceive to be merely relative, and incidental to our point of view."[69] Our conscience, said Martineau, shows us clearly that we live under an authority above us. The voice of conscience reflects what is ultimate. It instills in us the instinct of right and wrong and reminds us that we stand before the bar of an eternal and divine justice. Thus our faith that God is just grows from the depths of conscience, "and the Holiest that broods over us solemnly rises—the awful spirit of eternity—from the ocean of our moral nature."[70]

The moral intuition exists as certainly as God does, Martineau said, and we are under its divine command. We do, however, have the freedom to obey or disobey. Obedience raises us into divine relations with a wise, just, and holy God. Martineau said, "We have only to open and read the credentials of conscience, and this discovery bursts upon us at once. That sense of authority which pervades our moral nature, and tempers it with a silent reverence, places us under that which is higher than we. . . ."[71]

Indeed, for Martineau, moral consciousness is the highest part of our nature, and if we attend to it, we develop moral patterns of behavior. Memory, said Martineau, preserves our past acts, and our tendency is to repeat what we have done before. Yet experience can also teach us hard lessons, if we remember them. If we do not, conscience is easily compromised, and evil may appear attractive. Memory can also haunt us and cause sleepless nights: "Conscience cannot forget; and if it carries a criminal secret, it is so little able to bear the ill-deserts which have never been visited, that often, in order to force them to account, it will unbosom itself in confession after twenty or thirty years. Why does the sin thus refuse to die, long after it is physically worn out . . . ?"[72] In conclusion, Martineau believed that worship becomes more meaningful as we strengthen conscience and follow the moral law.

C. The Moral Law as Absolute

It is wrong, Martineau believed, to treat moral authority as an opinion or as grounded in one's cultural environment. Truth is the same for everyone. If opinion is the judge of morals, then one view is as good as another, and we approach a state of moral anarchy. Indeed, said Martineau, if the moral law is dependent on our attitude or view of life,

> it is equally justified in regard to intellectual truth which my nature constrains me to accept; and it would be only a proper self-restraint to say, "For my part, I think of space as having three dimensions; and I cannot think of two times as being together: but I speak only for myself, and have no right to expect assent from any one else...."[73]

Likewise, Martineau wrote: "It is no more possible that what would be evil in man should be good in God, than that a circle on earth should be a square in heaven."[74] That is, there is a universal law that is not arbitrary or humanly devised, but built into the very structure of things. Heaven and earth are bound by the same God and the same laws.

Thus, for Martineau, the moral law functioned in the same way as did physical laws. Were we to discover anywhere in the universe that the law of cause and effect did not hold universally, he wrote, or that events were not sequential, or that what caused a phenomenon one day did not do so the next day, all science would break down. It would be "a proclamation that creation had run wild,—that nature, relapsing into chaos, was knowable no more."[75] Just so, he said, if we found that sins were sometimes punished and sometimes not—if the saints were set with the wicked—that would be the death-knell of all moral faith. Martineau believed in punishment after death, but not eternal damnation—a punishment caused by our own guilt and ended when we change our understanding.

Martineau also thought that belief in a moral law was essential to healthy psychic functioning. The moral law must be firm, he said. How, he asked, could humanity sustain itself if we lived in an inconstant world amidst shifting elements, "whose rules & ways, gathered from the past, are not secure upon the future? Flexible laws would leave it ever doubtful whether God was really in earnest with us;—whether we need lay our hand vigorously to the task he sets, or not rather ask him for a holiday & hope that he will hold us excused."[76]

Thus, said Martineau, those who do not believe in the existence of a moral law might then conclude that there is no rule of justice, no fixed order in nature. From that premise arises the conclusion that human affairs are relative to time, place, and person, and that the strongest make the rules, "that life is all a scramble, whose prizes often go to the least scrupulous mind & the most greedy hand, & whose blanks are drawn, amid the laughter of the wise, by hesitating conscience & pious folly; & that there is nothing for it but that each man should help himself, & leave his neighbours to shift as they may."[77] In contrast, Martineau believed that we receive insights through conscience that are reliable and connect us with the divine. "No revelation could persuade me that what I revere as just, and good, and holy, is not venerable, any more than it could convince me that the midnight heavens are not sublime."[78]

Justice requires that sins be punished, both during life and after death, said Martineau: this is part of God's scheme for bringing betterment to individuals and thus humanity as a whole. The workings of the moral law, and its effects on our own lives, also teach us more of God than any intellectual study could do. Thus, said Martineau, the pure in heart shall see God. God rewards those who spend themselves in the service of humanity. Therefore, said Martineau, worship must appeal to the moral sense, because the moral sense inspires us to do our duty, thereby opening the window to God. Worship, Martineau said, seeks to ennoble the whole person, not just reform our attitudes or behavior. It must speak to us through various means: music, prayer, reflection, appeal to the mind and conscience, and reminders of our connection with other people and the rest of the world, but most of all reminders that we contain God within us. Martineau believed that worship can ennoble us but can also be a subtle lure into a prideful self-esteem. In addition, Martineau spoke out against the use of religion for utilitarian purposes. The moral law is not simply a device for the maintenance of social order; it is not a servant to be used when convenient or modified at will. The utilitarian view actually degrades religion when it promotes religion on the grounds that people are unmanageable without its restraints:

> It is a shameful spectacle, when its own representatives condescend to plead for it thus; and go ignominiously round, supplicating votes in its behalf, for the vacant office of Master of Police! What sort of obedience is likely to be rendered to a creature of our own appointment, chosen from prudence, and removable at pleasure? Nothing can be more evident than that such advocates are thinking only of restraining others, and by no means filled with the idea of submission themselves.[79]

Having rejected the moral law in its turn as a source of religious authority, Martineau then turned to the role of conscience.

5. Conscience
A. Conscience as the Key to Religion

One of the purposes of worship, said Martineau, is to strengthen our focus on and understanding of conscience, which is the primary source of our knowledge of God. Our imagination gives us our conception of God, he said, and conscience informs us of our communion with God. We heed our conscience not just to avoid censure or punishment, nor only to gain the pleasure of knowing that we have obeyed the dictates of God, but to be part of the Christian kingdom of love. If imagination tells us that duty exists, then conscience uses the idea of duty to bind us with God.

Thus Martineau believed conscience to be a binding authority. It prompts us, he said, to choose the better over the worse, right over wrong. It is the constant judge of our decisions; it tells us when we lapse into error, and it encourages us to act virtuously. Through our own will, we choose one option or another. Conscience appeals to us; we are ennobled by yielding to it and degraded by defying it. The warnings of conscience also remind us we will be disciplined for choosing wrongly. The conscience, as the voice of God within, reminds us that there is an invisible and superior voice without, appealing to our hearts.[80]

Conscience was the key to Martineau's religion; without it, he felt, his whole understanding of religion would collapse. Conscience, for

Martineau, is a reflection of both the holy that is within us and the moral nature of God. Just as with the moral law, if the dictates of conscience were transient, they would have no authority. Craufurd, who once called Martineau "this conscience-intoxicated Unitarian,"[81] wrote that if conscience were only relative, "Men might still find it convenient to use conscience as a kind of moral policeman; but they would no longer bow down before it as the viceregent of the Infinite and Eternal. Moral obligation would vanish, and be replaced by calculating prudence. . . . [T]he Cosmos in general might live in complete and disdainful indifference to our provincial ten commandments."[82]

On the contrary, said Martineau; the dictates of conscience reflect the eternal and unchanging will of God. There he found the answer that had eluded him. Conscience, said Martineau, is the primary authority for religion, and in fact he considered it the very source of religion, the communion between the individual and God, between the individual soul and the Universal Soul. He believed that conscience gave people the power to make independent judgments. Martineau said in his own ordination response that the minister "can receive no aid from the authority of any man, or any church. His most valuable guides are his own mind, and his own conscience; and his most valuable privilege in the use of these, is his unquestionable right of private judgment. Whether he study, or whether he teach, let him stand fast in the liberty wherewith Christ hath made him free."[83] Yet the person with conscience need not stand alone before God, but may join with others and receive sustenance from them. Indeed, said Martineau, it is dangerous to try to live the moral life outside of community: "he who is so lifted into a solitary position, as to have few equals and no apparent enemies, misses much of the invigorating discipline of life, and is perilously thrown on his own spontaneous faithfulness."[84]

Martineau was also interested in situations in which the authority of Scripture and the conscience were in conflict. Which, he asked, should prevail? His answer was that it depends on how we view human nature. Should we force scriptural authority on an unwilling mind? Is the mind, or the conscience, simply a passive receptor of religion, as the eye receives light? Are we to receive the truth handed down from the past and preserve it intact without question? No, Martineau insisted, religion is "rather a spontaneous element in human consciousness,—an instinctive wonder,—a prophetic watching of the full eye for light, so that God, when he comes, brings no surprise."[85] If we take religion as it has been handed down to us, the religion is not ours but someone else's. If truth is to be served, the conscience must be free to find its own way. Martineau tells us

> to restrain the sacred dove of the affections no longer in your narrow cage, but let it loose in the open skies, and see whither it beckons you away. Whoever can doubt that this is the lesson in accordance with the truth must, I think, be misled by a false philosophy, or deluded by a falser experience. Religion is more than an artificial product of mental instruction; it is the prayer of conscience, the vatication of reason, the natural faith of love. . . .[86]

Martineau's ideas on conscience as authority received plenty of challenges throughout his life. As discussed earlier, Martineau challenged the Unitarian reliance on Scripture as authority in his *Rationale of Religious Enquiry*, and he was the theologian who was most responsible for leading the Unitarians away from that standard. Martineau's substitution of conscience as authority occupied much of his later work, notably *Types of Ethical Theory* (1885), *A Study of Religion* (1888), and *The Seat of Authority in Religion* (1890). Yet, in his own lifetime, Martineau's ideas never won out entirely, and he struggled continuously both with himself and with the Unitarian movement, of which he became the leading theoretician. His repudiation of scriptural authority created a rift between him and the old-school Unitarians (which was, incidentally, thought to be the main reason he did not at first go with Manchester College when it moved to London).[87] Indeed, criticism of Martineau's position remained stern well into the 20th century. G. Dawes Hicks said in a 1936 speech at Manchester College that Martineau's position was weak because "having discarded the authority of the church and of the 39 Articles, having relinquished an appeal to the infallibility of the Scriptures or to a miraculous revelation as the ultimate ground of religious trust, it has no alternative but to fall back on crude individualism, according to which each man is his own Pope."[88]

B. The Authority of Conscience

For Martineau, then, conscience is the seat of all religious authority. It must instruct our beliefs and guide our worship. If worship is to bring us closer to God, it must do so by strengthening our understanding of the indwelling God. Each person has the task of harmonizing the teachings of Christ with the conscience and clearing up the confused rivalries of other sources of authority, insofar as possible, as far as the will and understanding direct. In this mission, he said, every person stands at the pinnacle of history—a lesson taught to us by Christ, the image and representative of God. Conscience, of course, is a heavy taskmaster, reminding us as it does of our lost opportunities, our vanished dreams, and all our sins, and telling us not only what has been but also what might be. Indeed, Martineau believed that conscience and sin were linked: "the insight of conscience and the sense of Sin are the source and not the fruit of religious fear."[89]

Both conscience and understanding, or perception, said Martineau, remind us of our divine nature. However, they conflict at one level. Conscience proclaims evil to be the antagonist of religion, while understanding proclaims it in fact to be the agent. That is, from the encounter with evil, the virtues are born. From the encounter with "the sickly seductions of pleasure," we learn the virtue of holiness; from the temptations of selfishness, we learn of self-denying love; from the temptations of hypocrisy, we learn to value honesty; and "So through anguish we learn pity; through our own failures we learn forbearance; through our grief, compassion. Scarcely can any ill be found that is not so linked with visible benefits."[90]

Martineau also sought to understand the relationship of conscience to reason. In his later thinking, Martineau dethroned reason as the chief authority, but he never denied its usefulness. The function of reason, he said, is to know and understand. Conscience has a different function: to help us discern our relations to the Good and to stimulate within us the sense of the divine. Reason and conscience prompt each other, giving us a stronger understanding of God. Likewise, conscience is the partner of justice; it is our judge not only in this life but also after death. Martineau believed that the logical extension of the moral law pointed to immortality, and that the consequences of our lives would follow us after death.

C. Conscience as the Voice of God

Conscience is the highest authority within us, said Martineau, but it derives from a still higher authority beyond us. There is within us a holy presence, he said, which links us together because it the same within all people. This "holy other" is the God beyond and external to us, who has placed our conscience within us. We know God through conscience, and we know that that the God within is not dependent on us, nor is it an invention of our imagination; it is independent of us, given to us to know and to apprehend. Thus Martineau believed conscience gave us a personal relationship with God, from which we derive our knowledge of the moral law.

Martineau pondered further the relationship between our experience of the moral law and in indwelling divinity, the sense of the holy. In summarizing his views on conscience, authority, duty, and will, he outlined four key points:

> 1. The Authority of Duty becomes transcendent and Divine. . . .
> 2. The Scope of Duty becomes for the first time co-extensive with the area of the Will. . . .
> 3. The Volume, or internal capacity, of the Moral Life is immeasurably expanded by gaining its religious interpretation. . . .
> 4. The Enthusiasm of the Moral Life is intensified by the consciousness of its Divine Source.[91]

In sum, said Martineau, conscience derives from God, not from socialization, early training, or education. We are in a world morally constituted, and we have within us the means of determining right and wrong: conscience, our highest authority. Of course, its guidance must be interpreted with reference to the current state of knowledge and social conditions. Yet the principle that conscience is fundamentally independent of society seemed obvious to Martineau:

> [The notion] that, if [the conscience] were not there at all, could society generate it, and, by skilful financing with the exchanges of pleasure and pain, could turn a sentient world into a moral one, will never cease to be an insolvent theory, which makes provision for no obligation: never, so long as it is true that out of nothing nothing comes. . . .
>
> No: skill and prudence are found; but conscience is given.[92]

Martineau stated this theme over and over again: "The wise and good of every age have variously struggled to express in adequate terms the solemnity of human obligation; but all the strivings of their thought have culminated in this: 'The word of conscience is the voice of God.'"[93]

> Conscience is [God's] revealer; through its activity do we know the Only Holy, who for ever makes the good the sole object of his choice and love. On man God has conferred the august privilege of sharing in this choice. Within the limitations of our humanity, he opens to us access to the infinite and eternal. He has so framed our nature that it can respond to his call.[94]

Thus Martineau worked his way through the major sources of authority over the mind, the authority that links us directly to God. In conscience he finally found the solution that had eluded him through his years of reflection. Martineau was an outstanding thinker in two related fields, philosophy and theology. Having settled his primary philosophical problem, the source of religious authority, he turned his attention to theology.

Notes

1. *Studies,* 179–96.
2. *Ibid.,* 193.
3. *The Seat of Authority,* 140.
4. *Ibid.,* 146.
5. *Ibid.,* 147–48.
6. *Ibid.,* 151.
7. *Ibid.,* 152.
8. *Ibid.,* 152.
9. *Studies,* 154.

10. *The Seat of Authority*, 152–55, 159.
11. The first and second editions appeared in 1836, the third in 1845, and the fourth in 1853.
12. *The Rationale of Religious Enquiry,* 72.
13. *The Rationale of Religious Enquiry,* 64.
14. *Ibid.*, 63–64.
15. Letter to Mr. Ireland, November 6, 1886, quoted in Drummond & Upton I, 93.
16. "Appendix" to "Loss or Gain in Recent Theology," 5.
17. *Hours I,* 298.
18. *Essays IV*, 34.
19. "Appendix" to "Loss or Gain in Recent Theology," 8.
20. *Hours II,* 96.
21. *Ibid.*, 96.
22. *Ibid.*, 349.
23. The criminal status of Unitarianism ended with the passage of the Dissenters' Chapels Bill in 1844; see Schulman, *Blasphemous and Wicked* for a detailed account of how Unitarianism achieved legal status in England.
24. *Essays IV*, 366.
25. *Essays IV*, 323.
26. *Ibid.*
27. "Appendix" to "Loss or Gain in Recent Theology," 3.
28. *Ibid.*
29. "What is Christianity? No. 8: Relation of Scripture History to Christianity, No 1."
30. *Ibid.*, 10–11, 14.
31. *Essays IV*, 68.
32. *Ibid.*, 2–3.
33. *Essays IV*, 294.
34. "The Bible: What It Is, and What It Is Not," 27–28.
35. *Ibid.*, 36f.
36. *Ibid.*, 42.
37. "Appendix" to "Loss and Gain in Recent Theology," 6.
38. *Essays IV*, 332.
39. *Essays IV*, 325.
40. "The Bible: What It Is, and What It Is Not," 3.
41. *Ibid.*, 6.
42. *Essays II*, 513–14; Luke 10.28.
43. *Essays II*, 526.
44. "Testimony of Christianity to the power of Human Affections," 9.
45. *Studies*, 195.
46. *National Duties*, 179–80.
47. *Ibid.*
48. "What is Christianity? No. 11: Relation of Belief to Character," 10.

49. *Essays IV*, 140.
50. *National Duties*, 184.
51. *Ibid.*, 184–85.
52. "Address by The Rev. James Martineau, delivered at The Soiree held in the Hope Street School-Room, Liverpool, September 25, 1871," 2.
53. *Ibid.*
54. *National Duties*, 2–3.
55. Drummond and Upton I, 231.
56. *Hymns of Praise and Prayer, Collected and edited by James Martineau, LL.D.*, x–xi.
57. "What is Christianity? No. 7: True Idea of a Revelation, No. 2," 6–7.
58. *The Seat of Authority in Religion*, 492.
59. "The Doctrine of Punishment," 8.
60. *Ibid.*
61. "Christian View of Moral Evil. A Lecture, Delivered in Paradise Street Chapel, Liverpool, on Tuesday, February 19, 1839," 47.
62. *National Duties*, 120.
63. *Hours II*, 30.
64. *Hours II*, 302.
65. *Ibid.*
66. "Christian View of Moral Evil ," 34–35.
67. *Essays IV*, 454.
68. *Types of Ethical Theory*, 2nd ed., 270.
69. *Studies*, 180.
70. *Studies*, 185.
71. *The Seat of Authority in Religion*, 71.
72. *Hours II*, 301.
73. *The Seat of Authority in Religion*, 65.
74. *Studies*, 189.
75. *Hours I*, 108.
76. *Essays III*, 8.
77. "Spirit of Christianity, No. 5: Providence, No. 1," 10.
78. *Studies*, 181.
79. *Endeavours*, 67.
80. *The Seat of Authority in Religion*, 57.
81. Craufurd, 192.
82. *Ibid.*, 57–58.
83. Carpenter, 66.
84. *Hours II*, 43.
85. *Hours II*, 314.
86. *Ibid.*, 317.
87. G. Dawes Hicks, quoted in *Encyclopaedia Britannica*, 14th ed., vol. 14, 981.

88. *Ibid.*
89. *The Seat of Authority in Religion*, 459.
90. "Christian View of Moral Evil," 10.
91. *Essays IV*, 307–9.
92. *The Seat of Authority in Religion*, 54–56.
93. *Ibid.*, 71.
94. Carpenter, 300.

Chapter V: Martineau's Theology

In the free churches, said Martineau, ministers must understand and be able to articulate in the context of worship the sources of their inspiration and their views on such important concepts as God, immortality, and Christ. Traditional churches use a prayer book, he explained, but free churches depend on the guidance of the minister and the customs of the local chapel. Accordingly, the leader must have both an understanding of liturgy and a theology that underpins it. Ministers do not have to agree with their colleagues on the doctrines that guide them, but each one must have a well-developed theoretical basis for worship. Otherwise, instead of directing congregants in the search for union with the divine, the liturgy becomes simply a collection of prayers, readings, and hymns without any clear pattern. This section discusses Martineau's own theology and its implications for his own worship, with particular attention to his understanding of human nature.

1. God
A. An Outline of Martineau's Thought

Martineau's understanding of worship rested on his theology. He wrote major works of systematic theology, which provide guides to meaningful worship. We will examine in turn his ideas about God, human nature, Jesus, his doctrine of the church, and his belief in immortality.

Worship for Martineau required a personal God because he believed an impersonal God was not a sufficient basis for ethics. Ethics are not the aim of worship, nor are they a substitute for it, said Martineau, but worship ought to have a direct effect on our lives. Ethics, he said, must be a consequence of belief in God, not a social contract or agreement among like-minded people, and God must speak to us in a personal relationship, not as an inference from nature or physical laws. Although God can speak to us in many ways, the strongest way is the direct link with conscience.

One of Martineau's contributions was to interpret philosophy and theology in terms of each other. Integrating his idealist philosophy into his theology, Martineau argued that human nature is close to God's and is part of the Absolute Mind.[1]

It is important to understand what Martineau meant by theology, since it was the basis for his theory of worship. Martineau once defined theology as "a knowledge or intelligent scheme of Divine things."[2] Elsewhere, he explained: "Theology is the doctrine of divine things; and for their true apprehension the theologian must station himself at the points where they manifestly touch the human and leave their mark within the range of our life and thought."[3] Many thinkers of Martineau's day divided theology into two branches, natural and revealed. To Martineau, both were important. Natural religion, he said, is that which we know through our reason and observation; revealed religion comes "by the gift of God, so close to the soul, so folded in with the very centre of the personal life."[4] Martineau compared the two in this way: "Natural religion is that in which man finds God; Revealed religion is that in which God finds man."[5] In the former, the human being is the thinking subject; in the latter, he writes, "The prime medium through which God descends upon our hearts & enters with his sanctity therein, is a spirit higher than our own. All men perceive by infallible instinct the presence of a greater and nobler mind. . . ."[6] That instinct, Martineau believed, lies at the core of worship.

The concepts of revealed and natural religion led Martineau to a belief in a personal God whose nature was reflected in human nature: "Shall I be deterred by the reproach of 'anthropomorphism'? If I am to see a ruling Power in the world, is it folly to prefer a man-like to a brute-like power, a seeing to a blind?"[7] God understood as a force of nature is not enough: "it was needful to have assurance that he lives. It was a poor thought that he was the beginning of all, if he stood aloof from it in its constancy."[8]

In the religious life, said Martineau, it is not a tenable theological position to worship a God removed from human striving or to live as if God were asleep or unconcerned. He believed that human efforts toward the good, just, and beautiful, valued as they are, are fragmentary until they are seen as unified in the love of God. We must go beyond the command to do good, be just, and show mercy, he said; we must also have a vision of how those qualities fit into a cosmic whole.

In fact, Martineau believed that it was self-evident that God is a governing force that rules over and cares for us. God is sensed through the highest of human striving, and this must be so, said Martineau. That human goodness reflects the divine is inherent in any meaningful concept of God: "Truth, justice, & goodness are eternally & intrinsically excellent, . . . & did he ordain anything different, he would thereby cease to be God, & become the tyrant instead of the divine Ruler of his creation."[9]

B. Science and God

Martineau was cautious about the effect of the expansion of scientific knowledge on religious understanding. In science, he saw a source of wonder, an opportunity for the elevation and advancement of the human spirit, and he used illustrations from science in his lectures and sermons. However, he worried that science provided so many physical explanations for nature that people might assume God to be less necessary: "[T]he expounders of the modern doctrine of natural development . . . apparently assume that growth dispenses with causation; so that if they can only set something growing, they may begin upon the edge of zero, and, by simply giving it time, find it on their return a universe complete."[10]

According to Martineau, it was also a mistake to assume that God was a force that had intervened in the world at some point, or had been important in the early stage of human culture, but was now no longer needed. The error in this way of thinking, said Martineau, is that God is not simply the first cause, but the indwelling principle that pervades the creation. When science tempts us to replace God with our own powers, we are distracted from God and, as it were, worship false idols: "if the lightnings could write upon the clouds 'We have no God, thou alone art divine,' into what ultimate horror would its dismal apotheosis plunge him!"[11] In fact, believed Martineau, although science and materialism seem to rob God of his powers, "this is a bare fiction of abstraction, shamming an integral reality,—an old soldier pensioned off from actual duty, but allowed to wear his uniform and look like what he was."[12]

Martineau also worried that the immensity of God across the universe revealed by modern science might make God seem less accessible than the obvious physical world. And he saw that science and its companions, industry and technology, could provide a seemingly endless supply of new inventions to absorb our attention and distract us from religious concerns with their promise of luxury and ease. But despite the fascinations of science, said Martineau, we must remember that it deals with the finite. The task of science, he said, is to attempt to describe and count everything in our vast universe. In this process, we must not forget that God is above all that is created

Some of these concerns played out in Martineau's reaction to the debate on evolution, one of the important disputes of his time. Martineau accepted evolutionary theory, but he felt that it tempted people toward a mechanistic view of the world: "it weakens our objective religion, suggests that there is no originating Mind, and that the divine look of the world is but the latest phase of its finished surface, instead of the incandescence of the inmost heart."[13]

Another important topic in Martineau's day was the age of the universe. It concerned both religious people, who may have followed Bishop Ussher in believing that the world was created in 4004 B.C., and people of science, who placed the date much earlier through their investigations of anthropology and archaeology. Martineau, however, rejected their research. He did not believe in a point when the world was created, before which it did not exist: "travel through the past with the most vigilant eye, you nowhere arrive at such event. The imagination of it is a pure fiction that begins and ends with the mind that thinks it. . . ."[14] Martineau also criticized the scientific image of God as the manufacturer of the universe, as if he were simply a cook mixing ingredients or an engineer constructing clouds, oceans, and planets. Martineau, in contrast, believed that God was the creator not just of the physical universe, but also of human nature and the moral law, the sustainer of life and the guarantor of truth and goodness.

In sum, Martineau saw that science could help in overcoming poverty and disease. He also recognized its fascination, its stimulus to the imagination. He himself was well read in science and used its illustrations often in lectures and sermons. But he also criticized the scientific worldview for tempting us to turn aside from religion, to seek answers to human problems without the concept of God. If there are so many disruptions to our sense of the indwelling God, then how do we understand God?

C. How God Is Revealed

According to Martineau, our belief in God is based on trust, not proof or examination of evidence: "The infinite Father does not stand by us to be catechised, and explain himself to our vain mind."[15] Belief begins with sensory stimulation. As children, we form ideas from our surroundings and interactions with others. Later our conscience and feelings confirm our religious beliefs. We first find evidence of God in the world without, said Martineau, and later feel the divine within. Martineau believed that worship should therefore encapsulate this pattern of development, beginning with an appeal to the senses; later, appealing to the will by hope and fear; and finally presenting God to us as love and trust. Worship recognizes that different people at different times come with varying moods and understandings. Worship must provide a variety of responses and approaches to accommodate those differing needs.

Religion is a reverence for something higher than ourselves, said Martineau, and we can discover this something because it is reflected within us; it is nobler than us and lifts us to a higher level. When we seek God through our senses and our understanding of physical laws, forces, and the relations between inanimate objects and processes, God appears to be impersonal. Seeking through the soul and conscience, on the other hand, leads us to the personal God that Martineau embraced.

For Martineau, the primary method of knowing God is through moral experience, intuition, and the moral order. As we reflect on our own spiritual nature, we expand our understanding to see the universe as like our own will and spirit, extended to infinity. We see God as we strive for the right, undertake works of charity, and exalt those higher qualities of the spirit that assure us we are part of something eternal and infinitely good. The reverse is true, too: "To one who dishonours himself by sloth and excess, God becomes invisible and incredible."[16]

Martineau saw God in the ordinary, not in obscure and rare events or in the lives of saints. He quoted the English physicist T. E. Poynting favorably:

> How often had a poor doubting mind confessed to me, "You say that God is in contact with us, and gives his Holy Spirit to those who ask Him. Yet I look back through all my life, and I am not aware of any inspiration, any revelation, any suggestion, that has not come, like all my thoughts and feelings, by my ordinary faculties and instincts. It seems to me that I have been left alone with my own mind, and God has not at all interfered in its workings." I now saw that what we call the ordinary working of the mind itself, the law of its faculties, the moving of its impulses, was the very flowing of the Holy Spirit.[17]

If God can be found in the ordinary, knowledge of God does not depend on our education, mental capacity, or cultural position. God can be found in every house and in every part of nature: in the cloud, sea, bird, and flower; in tenderness, joy, and grief; in striving after good; in love and caring for one another. "I do not think," Martineau said, "that we should discern him any more on the grass of Eden, or beneath the moonlight of Gethsemane."[18] We reflect God, as nature does; the divine purpose is seen and expressed throughout all that is created. For Martineau, the universe is the autobiography of God: "The grandest natural agencies are thus but servitors of a grander than themselves: 'the winds are his messengers; and flaming fire, his minister.'"[19]

D. The Personal God

Why did Martineau feel the need to believe in a personal God? Martineau believed the sense of God had disappeared from intimate experience and must be recovered. Martineau's stress on nature as the expression of God caused some to think he was a pantheist, but he denied the charge emphatically: "Am I asked whether this is not pantheism,—this identification of the dynamical life of the universe with God? I reply, it certainly would be so, if we also turned the proposition round, and identified God with no more than the life of the universe, and treated the two terms as for all purposes interchangeable."[20] The charge would be valid, Martineau said, if his own concept of immanency stopped there. But Martineau also stressed that God was transcendent, far more than the physical universe coupled with the laws that govern it. Martineau spoke of natural religion because he wanted to show people that they had more immediate access to God than through the usual means of creeds, hierarchies, and authorities. We may find God, he said, primarily within us, when we explore our own souls, but also in nature: "God . . . constructs a cosmos to be the mirror of his thought, covers it with greater and lesser circles of intersecting laws. . . ."[21]

Yet Martineau also saw how easily the theory of a personal God can be abused. He objected to people who claimed to know too much about God, who spoke as if they knew all God's plans and reasons and could interpret their own culture with reference to nothing but their understanding of God's will and plan for humanity. Such misguided convictions, wrote Martineau, "[throw me] into an indefinite agony of doubt, and impel me to cry, 'Ask of me less, and I shall give all.'"[22] In other words, Martineau advised us not to demand too much. We are close to God, but at the same time there is an infinite difference between God and us that requires our humility.

Yet the difference can be overcome. In fact, for Martineau, the premise that God is personal was a prerequisite for serious religious inquiry and commitment: "the Living God does really hold and always has held personal relations with every human being, and has constituted the soul for a responding life. . . ."[23] We fear to open ourselves to a personal God, Martineau said, because it goes against so much we have been taught and believe. We do well to be cautious, but we should follow the logic of the moral law and accept the idea that we really are connected with the divine powers that create, sustain, and govern the universe. God indeed is interested in us, said Martineau.

God possesses, wrote Martineau, "an all-embracing Love, an inexhaustible holiness, an eternal pity, an immeasurable freedom of affection, whence all the regularities of his will spring forth." Despite God's immensity and infinity, God still is so willed as "to visit the private wants of every soul, to linger with tenderness near every sorrow, to be present with rescue in every temptation. This it is that is the real ground of our trust and love: God is not merely the power of nature, but the Father of spirits. . . ."[24]

Thus, said Martineau, we are not alone in a cold and friendless world, and God is not only the creator of a vast universe; God numbers the very hairs on our head and deals with us individually, "not from the long perspective of creation, but here and here [sic], hour by hour, today & tomorrow, from morning to night. His Providence is no scientific disguise for the beneficence of Fate, but a living, watching, feeling Presence, open to pity & accessible to prayer."[25]

Moreover, said, Martineau, we do not rely on a God that merely spake of old. God still speaks if we will listen, he said—if we will pull aside from the distractions that tempt us. Our souls are as capable of receiving answers from God as any were in the past: "He was no nearer to Christ on Tabor or in Gethsemane, than to us this day and every day. . . . [E]very human being that is born is a first man, fresh in this creation, and as open to Heaven as if Eden were spread round him."[26] Here, the reference to Gethsemane reflects Martineau's belief that God speaks most clearly in our distress and suffering. God, he said, is nearest when we need him the most.

Further, said Martineau, we seek and can obtain union with God, a higher state than obedience to God. We may begin with obedience, but subservience can give way to a freer sense of harmony with God. This union or harmony is obtained through our conscience, "the handwriting of truth."[27] The pure in heart, Martineau believed, will see God after death. Through our holiness we imitate Christ and become with him disciples of God, allowing God's will to guide us in our affections and duties. This does not mean that we must invite God into us; God is already within us, and we can either recognize or ignore that divinity. It was important to Martineau that we see God not just in nature, or in the tides of history, or even in humankind, but within ourselves as well as in the people we encounter.

A divine potential belongs to us all, said Martineau, not just to the saints or those of extraordinary gifts. If we open ourselves to the possibilities of the religious life, we will see evidence of the indwelling God:

> When we feel the impulse of Benevolence, the love of the Beautiful, the love of Knowledge, when we feel the Sentiment of Conscience, approving or disapproving, when we feel the reason leading us on from step to step of truth we know not how,—whence do these impulses and movings come? What is their fountain? Do we invent these movements? Do we originate or direct them ourselves? No, the movements seem to come in upon us like streams of life from a source outside our Will. Now what is the source from which these streams or movements come?[28]

Those promptings come from within us. Yet that is not to say that we each have a cache of wisdom waiting to be opened, a treasure to be found and unlocked, that comes from ourselves alone; the source is God himself speaking to us. To Martineau, God is not just a presence, but the indwelling life; not a disembodied intellect, but a penetrating will that guides individuals as well as the universe. God is not a distant law that makes its ethical demands, but "an almighty wind that sweeps wherever spirits are."[29] God, like that wind, penetrates everywhere that is open to such influence. God, said Martineau, is ever-present; we always have access to God. This access to the divine, Martineau believed, is what makes our hearts ache for another who is suffering, provides our noble aspirations, shows us beauty, and chastens us when necessary. He writes: "Godliness is the persistent living out of an ideal preconception of the Right, the Beautiful, the Good."[30] And elsewhere:

> If the secret passages of our life could be laid open, where would be found those hours of purest consecration, the moments of clear faith, of open love, of willing duty, of felt envelopment in God? . . . [W]hen you stood before some being to whom you looked up as nobler, purer, simpler than yourself. This it is that reaches at once the springs of real

devotion in the soul, & sprinkles us with the wave of true regeneration.³¹

Thus, said Martineau, we must be open to such inspiration as comes, as in silent prayer we allow thoughts to flow into us. Martineau did not, however, advocate a passive reception of inspiration. He urged people to accept the implications of their connection with God. That led him to a consideration of the nature of duty that ought to flow from worship.

E. Duty

For Martineau, duty is a consequence of worship, not a substitute for it. Duty must be guided by theology: "Where there is no quieting perception of a Divine Presence in the world, the sense of justice, the indignation at wrong, sinks into a revolutionary passion, fantastic in its speech and reckless in its ways, instead of a grave and considerate obedience to the eternal Law of God."³²

One problem with duty, said Martineau, is that people rightly take it seriously but mistake it for the primary function of religion, rather than an adjunct. Some say religion is how we live, but Martineau said that religion is what we are. Martineau drew a distinction between different religions: "To give him something that we have is Heathen; to offer what we do, is Jewish; to surrender to him what we are, is Christian."³³ That is, in his formulation, heathens offer their goods to God in atonement; Jews strive for righteousness in fulfillment of their covenant with God; Christians surrender their will in communion. The first way attempts reconciliation by sacrifice, the second by obedience to God's laws, the third by loving self-abandonment and union with God's perfection. Clearly, Martineau considered Christianity the superior way.

Yet Martineau also believed that the third step must follow after the first two. We must give of our goods and of ourselves, thus performing our duties. Our sense of duty, said Martineau, is placed in us by God as a vision of a purer and more nearly perfect order, one that we can help achieve. It calls us to relinquish our love of ease and to heed the cry of those who need our help. In his charge to Alexander Gordon as Minister of Hope Street Chapel, Martineau said, "The approach to God is not the lonely path of untrodden thought, but the well-worn way of love; and the more you take the yoke of burdens not your own . . . , the more patient care you bestow in opening the faith and conscience of the young . . . , the fresher and the fuller will be your store of wisdom from above, and the truer your vision of Him whom the pure in heart shall see."[34]

In sum, said Martineau, Christianity is built on serving others, righting wrongs, and following the precepts of Jesus to give food to the hungry, drink to the thirsty, and care for those denied a stake in their culture, those who are in grief and burdened by the world. God requires the Christian to perform these duties, as one aspect of the path leading to God. Duty, then, is a necessary consequence of devotion. But what is there about us that impels us to such duty?

2. Human Nature
A. The Human as Incarnation

Nothing so distinguished Martineau from his contemporaries as did his doctrine of human nature. Martineau believed that we are all incarnations of God, just as Jesus was: "The Divineness which I claim for Jesus is no other than that which I recognise in every human soul which realises its possible communion with the Heavenly Father. And the preeminence which I ascribe to him is simply one of degree; so superlative, however, as to stand out in strong relief from the plane of ordinary history."[35]

Martineau rejected the Christian tradition that held that humanity and God are hopelessly estranged from one another. On the contrary, he said, we embody God: "The worlds he made out of nothing; but man out of himself: the one, accordingly, he has put under necessity; the other he draws with cords of love."[36] We are part of God now, not just after death. God is present in us through our conscience, said Martineau; as we recognize that divine conscience, our excessive concern with sensual pleasure falls away, and we are led by the spirit of God. Thus we claim divinity with Jesus. We are aware that we embody God, Martineau believed, because our goodness imitates God and our wisdom is from God. We are holy because we are not merely created by God; we are God's children.[37]

And God is in our very being, in our highest affections and our greatest generosity. The difference between Christ and us is that divinity permeated Christ's whole being, whereas in us it is partial, struggling for the completion that Christ knew.

Thus Martineau thought that we literally embody the divine: "Man is himself a cause; different in scale, indeed, from the Creator; but resembling him in capacity to perceive the same distinctions between good and evil. These are no products of our pleasures and pains; they have their roots in the Eternal Mind."[38] To apprehend God is to realize our own highest nature, and union with God is self-reconciliation.

Accordingly, said Martineau, when we do what is right and shun what is wrong, we feel ourselves closer to the divine. We are aware that God looks with favor on our generous acts, our deeds of love, and our succor of the lonely and grieving, as God looks with aversion on our greed, pride, and cowardice. When we meditate on the divine, said Martineau, we are disgusted with our own selfishness and criminal passions—our urges that result from greed, lust, and envy, and our excessive sensual appetites. Such disgust is a rebuke from God. That is, God as judge is within us, approving and disapproving: "Our moral nature, left to itself, intuitively believes that guilt is an estrangement from God,—an unqualified opposition to his will,—a literal service of the enemy; that he abhors it, and will give it no rest till it is driven from his presence, that is, into annihilation."[39] In our quiet times, said Martineau, we feel the promptings of a diviner life. We have a consciousness, vague though it may be, of a nobler calling than we have yet followed; we feel a dissatisfaction with our past ways, and we know we can do better. We feel a desire to cast out the poison that infects our spirit, a longing for the goodness that has eluded us. Beauty and joy have thus far been out of reach. Yet we can attain them by reflecting on ourselves as containing the divine, as creatures capable of beauty, generosity, love, and trust—qualities that are encouraged by worship. These promptings, Martineau said, are "the touch of God upon us; his heavy hand laid upon our conscience, and felt by all who are not numb with the paralytic twist of sin."[40]

B. Temptations

Martineau believed that humans had progressed because they were dissatisfied with their circumstances and yearned for something better for themselves and for others. Acquisitiveness, he said, has served us both well and ill, and it must be controlled. We are governed by the opposing principles of pleasure and nobility, and we are too often distracted from the noble and true by evil forces, said Martineau. We are tempted and tyrannized by the goods of the world. Habits form that distract us from the consciousness of God and our spiritual nature. Much in life can make us cynical, particularly our inclination toward indulgence of the passions and our love of enjoyment. Sensualism, because it is a source of immediate pleasure, is easily abused. That is, we are easily led to pamper ourselves and neglect duty toward others, the second of Jesus' two commandments. Thus, sensualism becomes a substitute for worthy strivings, for the sense of having contributed to human betterment and having striven for the truth that comes to the devout. Luxury makes us selfish, "where no love lingers and tears only pretend to flow."[41] For one who falls victim to such temptations, "The saintly words of everlasting hope will be as a strange jargon in his ears: the death-rattle on the bed will put out all the silent possibilities of eternity: he will shake off the remembrance of them as the remnants of a troubled dream; and return, with a shrug, to the table of his enjoyment, to 'eat and drink, since tomorrow he dies.'"[42]

"There is no hell so far from God, no exile so total, as the cares of sordid self-interest," Martineau wrote,[43] and he devoted much energy to tracing why humans succumb to this "sordid self-interest." One reason we succumb to temptation, he said, is that science reminds us continually of our affinity with other animal species, leading us to forget our spiritual nature. Science, said Martineau, fascinates us with its imagination and its continual expanding the boundaries of knowledge. It has cured so many problems that we come to believe it can solve *all* problems. There are two dangers here: on the one hand, that we will become too fascinated with trinkets; on the other, that we will turn away from those problems that science cannot cure. In fact, Martineau believed our deepest problems are those that science does not control: the sense of aimlessness, our grief, emotional separation from each other, and failure to have adequate goals or to live up to those who have.

In addition, the love of ease and the fear of ridicule debase us and sap our moral earnestness, causing us to shrink from difficult tasks and convince ourselves that nothing is worth fighting for anyway. We persuade ourselves that we really have no foe; then sacrifice and service are set aside, and the Christian life is compromised. Our true foes, said Martineau, are internal: our wishes to retreat from the hard side of life, to avoid situations that may cause us hardship or grief, to turn away from those who need our help, and to persuade ourselves to be content with our inadequate strivings. The love of ease, said Martineau, results partly from our failure to foresee the consequences of action or inaction: "In prospect, nothing appears so attractive as ease and licensed comfort; in retrospect, nothing so delightful as toil and strenuous service. Half the actions of mankind are for the diminution of labour; yet labour is the thing they most universally respect."[44]

We may then easily drift without purpose, said Martineau, with no greater care than transitory pleasures. We pick our companions accordingly, avoiding those who know more or see deeper and surrounding ourselves with those who will confirm our prejudices and who will not trouble our consciences—with "slaves . . . who either have nothing which they revere, or, having it, insult its authority, and trample it under the Bacchanalian feet of pleasure."[45] And so, said Martineau, we may fall into self-contempt because we love pleasure, fame, or wealth more than God.

Yet it need not be so. At their best, religious people have ideals that they cherish more than self-indulgence. They wage within themselves a holy war against the encroachments of evil, said Martineau; as they battle evil, self-denial becomes a privilege, not a loss; a victory, not a defeat. To such people, even hardship and death are honorable and welcome. "Some men," said Martineau, "are eminent for what they possess: others, for what they achieve: others, for what they are. Having, Doing, and Being, constitute the three great distinctions of mankind, and the three great functions of their life. . . . To get good, is animal: to do good, is human: to be good, is divine."[46]

With this understanding of human nature, Martineau turned his attention to one of the problems which he saw crippling human efforts: suffering.

C. Suffering

Martineau saw suffering as a path to understanding God but also believed that worship helps us understand, combat, and reconcile ourselves to suffering. To understand the role of suffering, he said, we must recognize that happiness is not a sufficient goal for human existence. Reason, conscience, devotion to truth, and depth of love are goods greater than pleasure, ease, or even rapture: "No, it is the heart of morbid & unfaithful ease that makes insatiable demands for happiness as the condition of its trust, & the more you gratify it, the more it refuses to believe."[47] In fact, said Martineau, if our faith is strong, suffering can become a source of strength. It is natural, he said, for us to want what is pleasant, easy, and rewarding, and to avoid what is unlovely, harsh, and repulsive. It is also natural to think of suffering as a painful part of life, an unwelcome intrusion into an ordered existence. It seems to us a spiritual or at least an emotional deformity, something to be cast off or exorcised. Yet that is not how God made the world, Martineau said. Our two natures, animal and spiritual, conflict with each other, and we must not judge situations by how much they satisfy our animal nature, but by what they do to the human spirit. According to Martineau, "Pain & sorrow are not accidents to be slurred over or run through; they are radical elements in our existence, that never fail to ripen their sweet or bitter fruits in every lot."[48] Thus suffering can be a source of strength, or it can crush us. Like Antaeus, we can be strengthened by every defeat; or like Job, suffering can cause us to question God's wisdom.

Those who want to get through life without pain and suffering are asking the impossible. Indeed, said Martineau, considering that we would become spiritually weak and emotionally impoverished if we were shielded from all harm and unpleasantness, ease is not in the least desirable. Martineau was at his tenderest and most eloquent when he spoke of grief and sorrow, as in this sermon:

> How few the years that pass over any house, without giving its inmates some object of tenderness & self-denial! How rare the minds that in their sunniest atmosphere, carry not their speck of cloud! Unable to forget these things, the devout disciple quietly provides a place for sorrow. When it knocks at the gate he opens to it immediately & deals hospitably with the sad messenger of God. So far from being taken by surprise, as though trouble had no right to come, he would almost suspect something wrong if he had no cross to bear; & pray that he might not fall away for want of chastening love. I know of no attitude more characteristic of the Christian than this free clasping of the thorns & folding them upon the heart.[49]

Thus the disciple of Christ understands that sorrow is "the sad messenger of God," a kind of "chastening love." If the world had no supply of agony, we would have no heroes or saints. The suffering of Christ caused the Roman centurion to confess him to be a Son of God. The moral structure of the universe, said Martineau, is such that suffering inspires us to create, shows us the need to love, and urges us to join in community. Suffering binds us together in our search for God, and worship must take its message into account. Worship must help us see the religious use of suffering—that it brings us closer to the heart of God—so that we do not see suffering as punishment or the curse of Fate, but as a direct means to understand the workings of God. In sum, said Martineau, God allows suffering because it lets us test and prove our courage.

D. The Dual Nature of Humanity

Martineau believed that humans have a dual nature, and he was disgusted with religions that saw only one side of humanity, "whether the Church [of England] whines to him about human depravity, or Socinianism repeats its platitudes on human dignity."[50] The Unitarians followed mostly the Socinian approach,[51] and Martineau felt its optimism did not attend sufficiently to the reality of evil: "One says that man is a brute; another, that he is an angel; the fact is, that he is both."[52] Our nature is merciful, loving, kind, and compassionate, said Martineau, but it is also selfish, resentful, envious, and proud.

Our nature has another dichotomy, too, said Martineau: we consist of body and soul. "We are the theater," he wrote, "on which the physical and the spiritual meet, and, through antagonism, struggle into unity."[53] One part of us relates to the world of experience and physical objects. Its tendency is to live primarily in that world, considering anything outside of it as a fiction, or at best superficial. Yet within each of us there is also a nature that is related to the Infinite. The first nature produces our science, skill, and prudence; the second, our philosophy, poetry, and reverence for duty. In Martineau's view, "It is a shallow mind which . . . is conscious of nothing but what it can measure in evidence and state in words."[54]

What, asked Martineau, is our true nature? Martineau believed humans are superior to other species, but in what way? Does human superiority consist in a more highly developed mechanical sense, a more complex brain, and the ability to provide the physical necessities more easily than lower animals? If so, we may head the roster of animals, but we are no closer to God. For Martineau, the best part of our nature lay in our appreciation of beauty, our sense of wonder, our desire to help one another, and, most of all, our search for God. He pointed out that it is universally considered contemptible for people to squander their intelligence on base pursuits, to live off the earnings of others, or to fail to contribute to human welfare and the alleviation of suffering. And we value most highly those qualities that, in fact, do not aid physical well-being. So are we brute or angel? Both, replied Martineau:

> With faculties ranging through the whole interval between animal & the divine, there are actual contrarieties in himself, struggles between irreconcilable principles, an alternate ascendency of the vile & the noble, appetite now insatiable & monstrous, now forgotten & extinct, here an out-blaze as from hell below, of fiery passion, there, a diffusion, as from heaven above, of sweet & sunny affections. . . .[55]

One important function of Christian worship, said Martineau, is to lead us from the brutish to the divine. The brutish cannot be set aside entirely, and it lies always in wait; but it can be subdued by a sanctified life. When we withdraw from God, human nature degenerates, but through communion with the innate and external Deity we become holy and noble. The brute is tamed, and through prayer we emerge from the darkness of our animal nature into the light of our spiritual nature.

3. Jesus
A. Martineau's Christology

As previously noted, Martineau firmly believed that ministers must be representatives of Christ; being a theist was not enough. Although Martineau had a broad concept of allegiance to Christ, he did believe that ministers must worship in Christ's name and spirit, according to their own understanding. Jesus, said Martineau, contained God to the highest degree attained by any human, and we need to acknowledge the superior sense of deity that Jesus attained as a pattern for ourselves. Jesus was the author of Martineau's religion, and Martineau's own reliance on the person and example of Jesus never wavered. As Waller noted, 143 of Martineau's 187 published sermons were about either Christ's person or his monitions.[56] Although Christianity centers on the person of Jesus as the manifestation of the divine in humanity, Martineau said, it is unclear to what extent Jesus was divine and how far he typified human nature. The New Testament has so many representations of Jesus. Which is the true one? Is it the one portrayed by Matthew, Paul, or John? Do we find the real Jesus in his parables and ethical teachings or in the mysticism of John's gospel? This issue is important, said Martineau, because the surrounding confusion can weaken our allegiance to what Jesus stood for.

Jesus, said Martineau, showed us the possibilities of allowing God to perfect us. But Martineau belived we must undertake that task ourselves; we must not expect Jesus to do it for us: "We cannot allow the Conscience to resign for an instant its native right of immediate contact and audience with God: to delegate the privilege is treason; and to quit his eye is death."[57] Jesus was devoted entirely to God and thus opened himself to a beatific vision. As we do likewise, said Martineau, we have fellowship with Christ: his Father becomes our Father, too. Thus, Jesus has revealed to us an example of devotion to God that can strengthen our own consciences to become one with God.

Martineau believed that it was the perfection of Jesus' moral and spiritual nature that caused God to dwell so completely in him. But Martineau was not always clear on which of Jesus' contributions made him worthy of the high honors paid him. Was Jesus an exemplar? Did he bring new teachings? Was it his character that made him important? If so, what did he exemplify, what were his new teachings, what about his character was critical?

Jesus has spiritual power for us, said Martineau, not only because of his teachings or his example, nor even because of anything that set him apart from us, but primarily because his example inspires us to seek the union with God that is our true nature. So, said Waller, Christ for Martineau reveals both humanity and God, what we are and what we can be.[58] Christ represents the highest form of humanity. Jesus is then a "perfect vision" who arouses us to the ideals inherent in our hearts.[59] He is the representative of God who shows us our true spiritual nature.

But how did Jesus think of himself? According to Martineau Jesus, as reported in the gospels, varied in his thought about his relation to God. Martineau was delighted by the considerable research on this topic done during his lifetime in higher criticism.

Martineau was also interested in the way Jesus was transformed from the "son of Man" into the "son of God." Jesus spoke of himself as "son of Man," a phrase implying self-surrender and humility. This image was far from the Messianic grandeur expected by people in Jesus' day and granted to him later. Jesus was the man who asked, "Why callest thou me good?" He was a man of sorrows, not the heir to David's throne, a man who knew temptation and forgave temptation in others, whose mission was to the poor and disenfranchised. He found his comfort in the inner life, not in outward possessions: "So foxes have holes and birds of the air have nests; but the Son of Man has nowhere to lay his head." He told the rich young ruler to sell all he had if he would be a disciple. Jesus the "son of Man" did not make any Messianic claim during his lifetime

It was only later, between the death of Jesus and the fall of the Jewish state, said Martineau, that the term "son of Man" came to be used in the Messianic sense and was then transformed into "son of God," a term that came to refer to Jesus' heavenly nature. Then, said Martineau, the gospel writers spread the myth that Jesus was the unique "son of God" by writing accounts of how the evil spirits that he exorcised recognized him as the holy one of God and addressed him as "son of God." Martineau reiterated, however, that this title was not used by those who knew Jesus, nor by Jesus himself. So, according to Martineau, Jesus did not claim to be, nor did Martineau recognize him as, the Messiah.

B. The Nature of Jesus

In Martineau's view, Jesus was an inspired human incarnated by God, just as every person is incarnated by God. Jesus did not have exclusive claim to the title "son of God":

> Him we accept, not indeed as very God, but as the true image of God, commissioned to show what no written doctrinal record could declare, the entire moral perfections of Deity. . . . The peculiar office of Christ is to supply a new moral image of Providence; and everything, therefore, except the moral complexion of his mind, we leave behind as human and historical merely, and apply to no religious use.[60]

The elevation of Jesus to Messiah, Martineau stressed, came after his death and as a consequence of disappointment by the Apostles. Their expectations of his being the Messiah were not fulfilled during his life; he had not ushered in the kingdom of God nor brought about the reign of peace, love, and justice. Thus, said Martineau, "To discuss whether Jesus was the Messiah, is even more unmeaning than the question whether John the Baptist were Elijah; for Elijah was at least a person, but Messiah was only a conception."[61] Therefore, Martineau said, by claiming that Jesus was the Messiah, the first-century Christians set up the chief error of Judaic theology as the primary tenet of Christianity.

Martineau considered Jesus to be a real person with a human nature influenced by a particular cultural context. He did not even accept the use of the title "Lord" for Jesus. According to Drummond, "Dr. Martineau objected strongly to the use of that term, because he thought it implied quite a false moral relation, reducing men to the condition of slaves, with no conscience, judgment, or will of their own, and that this relation of master and slave was denoted by its primitive use."[62] Nor did Martineau credit Jesus with intellectual infallibility. Jesus grew up within the culture of first-century Palestine. He developed amid that particular culture, though he was critical of much of the Judaism of his day and possessed a strong conscience and great sympathy for the poor, the lonely, and the wretched—even those outside his own tribe or religious group. Martineau said, "Our rule requires from him no intellectual infallibility, no exemption from all influences of an early home, of human ties, of rational thought, of the oriental atmosphere of life. He was actually in these relationships; with human eyes he looked round upon them; with human affections he loved them."[63]

On the other hand, Martineau did credit Jesus with a unique divine mission: "it is fit that, amid the diversities of partial examples and ideals, there should be one outward standard of all that is sacred and holy; that once in history God should not simply visit a soul, but wholly occupy it."[64] Jesus experienced the temptations and weaknesses of humanity, but he was obedient, dependent, and capable of suffering in his acceptance of God; we can be like him. Thus, said Martineau, "The Man of Sorrows is our personal exemplar; the Son of God is our spiritual ideal."[65] Elsewhere he added, "once in history, He who lives in us in proportion to our purity of heart, did entirely occupy a human soul, so as to express through it his love, his pity, and the beauty of his holiness; when we say that, as the heavens declare the dimensions of his outer glory, the Son of Man shows forth the colour of his inner spirit."[66]

Martineau believed Jesus' appeal in his own day must have been due, in large part, to the suffering experienced by his fellow Jews. In his day, the Romans subjugated Jews, corruption was rife in government and religion, and evil was writ large, but Jesus represented the image of humanity carrying divine insight and offering reprieve from the sorrows and burdens the people faced. Only from such a God-possessed man, said Martineau, could the monition "Be ye therefore perfect, even as your

Father which is in heaven is perfect"[67] be accepted without irony. Jesus meant not that we should be self-conscious before God, but that we should live as God would have us live. So, said Martineau, "from him we accept the injunction, as giving not only the ideal of our life, but the actual of his."[68]

C. The Religion of, Not about, Jesus

Along with most Unitarians of his day, Martineau believed that Christianity should be the religion of Jesus rather than a religion about Jesus. The common belief among the Unitarians was that we should believe everything that Jesus plainly taught. As previously discussed, Martineau partially demurred in recognizing that some parts of Scripture cannot be reconciled with other parts. An understanding of Jesus required a critical understanding of the Bible, which meant accepting some parts and rejecting others, and critically reflecting on the meaning of passages. In such cases, reason must be used, and therefore reason is superior to Scripture. Martineau was well-versed in biblical criticism and did not accept the Scriptures at face value. However, he agreed with the Unitarians in subscribing to the teachings of Jesus, and, as the next section will explore, he worked to sort out what those teachings were.

Martineau was unhappy that Christianity had veered away from the religion of Jesus, instead substituting a theory about Jesus:

> [W]hat he was in nature, what he did by coming into the world, what he left behind when he quitted it. These are the matters of which chiefly confessions and churches speak; and, by doing so, they make him into the object, instead of the vehicle and source of their religion; they change him from the "author," because supreme example, into the end of faith; and thus turn him, whose very function it was to leave us alone with God, into the idol and the incense which interpose to hide him.[69]

That error works against the intention of Jesus, which was to teach us about union with God and the duties deriving from that union. Thus, said Martineau, Christianity has actually frustrated what Jesus intended by building up a mythology about him. Martineau traced the changes in the Christian understanding of Jesus: the disciples made him into the Jewish ideal, or Messiah; then Paul transformed him into the second Adam (Martineau noted that Paul always called Jesus "son of God," never "son of Man," which has entirely different connotations); finally, through the influence of the Gospel of John he was changed into the incarnated son of God. These successive false transformations clouded his earthly ministry.

Martineau recognized, however, that such transitions were natural. As time passed and memories of Jesus faded, the people in their reverence for him imagined a more ideal version of Jesus than he himself had intended or than his disciples had known. The simplicity of his life among them faded. Yet in this process, said Martineau, the real Jesus had been lost. Thus Martineau called for a renewed focus on what Jesus believed in order to learn to follow his example:

> While therefore I distinctly profess discipleship to Christ, & derive little & less hope from any natural religion either of philosophy or of sentiment without him; while I embrace an interpretation of life & death, of the human lot & obligations, of the divine Nature & Providence . . . ; I yet take my vow, not to his theology, but to his religion [that is, not to his beliefs but to his inspiration from God].[70]

Martineau's reasoning here is surprising. When we focus on the teachings of Jesus, said Martineau, we find the divine; in the teachings about him we find the human. The teachings of Jesus show us what he was, his spiritual character and his moral relation to God. Theology—teachings about Jesus—is what others thought about Jesus' person and function:

> It was the Providence of history that gave us him: it was the men of history that dressed up the theory of him: and till we compel the latter to stand aside, and let us through to look upon his living face, we can never seize the permanent essence of the gift. By a standing delusion of theological egotism . . . Christianity has been taken to mean, not the religion of Jesus Christ, but some doctrine about Christ.[72]

For Martineau, then, the essence of Christianity is the religion of Jesus. Yet Martineau did not fully embrace everything that Jesus believed, because he saw Jesus as a man of his own time and place, a man who dealt with many problems and traditions of his day that now are obsolete. This fact, however, does not make Jesus less real or less important? It did not matter to Martineau that Jesus was not the "son of David": "Is his ministry of love and power no longer a suasion 'external to us,' though no prophet knew it beforehand? Is Gethsemane dumb and has Calvary vanished, because they are only in history to speak for themselves, and not thrust into dogma to speak for them?"[72] By stressing Christianity as it derives from Jesus' teachings, Martineau believed, worship prepares us for union with God. Then what were the teachings of Jesus that Martineau considered paramount?

D. What Jesus Taught

In teaching, Jesus used metaphor, parable, and hyperbole. He taught great truths, incapable of being expressed in ordinary speech, because he dealt with the souls of people. For Martineau, the primary message of Jesus was, "The Kingdom of Heaven is at hand." Jesus, said Martineau, lived in a time of growing apprehension that the present epoch was about to end, and he sensed a divine crisis that would require a new spiritual birth in all people. The Kingdom would be a reign of truth and righteousness, a promise made to the patriarchs of Israel that was now approaching fulfillment. Yet, said Martineau, Jesus himself did not claim that he would be the person to bring about or rule over the new Kingdom. His task was to announce it, warn of it, and prepare people for it.[73]

Jesus intended by his life and teachings, said Martineau, "not to persuade the Father, not to appease the Father, not to make a sanguinary purchase from the Father, but simply to 'show us the Father.'"[74] Jesus wanted to change the emphasis of the Judaism of his time from a concern for correct form into an awareness that God is within the soul, to teach people (in Martineau's words) that they are not here as outline shadows of the past, but as fast-living realities of the present gifted with awful dimensions of Freewill . . . to give them an open heart of simplicity & love, to glorify & bless their immediate being, instead of idly waiting till some fire of God shall consume the dead fuel of their dull life; these were the great ends for which the prophet of Nazareth lived, & wept, & prayed, & died.[75]

Jesus, said Martineau, was a prophet. He wanted to return to the people private religion and disengage it "from the encumbrances that stifle all its power; to re-awaken it from its sleep within our nature; to fill us with courage to trust in it; to dissipate the crowd of false reliances, & leave us once more alone with God."[76] Jesus, and Martineau in his turn, sought to awaken the people from a soporific religion of creeds, catechisms, and Articles of Faith. Jesus, said Martineau, sought to make the invisible world visible and give an infinite feeling of God a finite shape; thus would worship become a vital force in our lives.

For Martineau, Jesus was an ethical exemplar, but he was also much more than that. His work was divine—not just the effort of one man, but of God, and even more inspiring than instructive, "possessing the soul, guiding the will, subduing the conscience; every way exercising that mysterious power by which the greater holds the lesser nature, as in the hollow of the hand."[77] Ethics, said Martineau, is our great prayer to God, the measure of our wish for the kingdom of the righteous to come.

Jesus, said Martineau, had found God inside himself, a kingdom of heaven within that could be nurtured to help him know and do God's will. He demonstrated that to others so that they could know the fruits of holiness, too. God thereby became for Jesus not just the Creator, but the Redeemer and Sanctifier. That is, for Martineau, to be redeemed and sanctified meant to know God within and do God's will. God is immediate and immanent, said Martineau, and Jesus "had this peculiarity: that he plunges us into the feeling, that God acts not there but here; not was once, but is now; dwells, not without us, like a dreadful sentinel, but within us, as a heavenly spirit, befriending us in weakness, and bracing us for conflict."[78]

4. Ecclesiology

Martineau's ecclesiology, already introduced in the discussion of Martineau's views on the ministry, now needs to be set in the wider context of his theology.

Martineau taught that the Church is a metaphorical body that contains the spirit of Christ. Here, the Church is the body of all those Christians who worship sincerely and who are devoted to holiness—"the invisible church," as opposed to the visible church of various organizations. The Church is one universal body, and the local society or denomination is part of that body in communion with other gatherings. The Church is a holy institution because it embodies and points toward the divine; holy also because therefore its focus is away from the secular (despite its many worldly concerns); and holy because it points toward eternity rather than the temporal. It strives to be and is, at its best, the visible Kingdom of God. The Church in essence is an invisible body, with the actual membership known only to God. We join the visible church and hope that through our faith we are also part of the invisible church.

Who, then, are members of the church? Martineau answered: all who claim Christ as the highest incarnation of God and who want to be included. Yet he set some requirements: to be a Christian, one must believe first in the historicity of Christ; second, in Christ as the highest and most nearly complete incarnation of God; and third, that there was something supernatural in Christ. This point is discussed further in Section D, below.

The Church, according to Martineau, is placed in history, but it also transcends history by the indwelling of God's spirit. It transcends distance because it is universal and unlimited in time. The true Church is where God's spirit is found.

What would such a church be like? Martineau wanted a church based on the Apostolic vision, but not uncritically so. The early Church was closer in time and thought to the mind of Christ, but it was also a product of its own culture.

A. Defining the Church

Martineau's emphasis on the individual connection with God tended to de-emphasize the role of the Church. He was not a sacramentalist. He did not believe God is present in physical objects; rather, he believed that the rites of the church are important symbols that remind us of our need for grace and show us how to obtain it, but do not impart it. A person is not saved by baptism or other symbols, he said, nor condemned without them. These symbols, he said, are valuable only insofar as they stir in us consciousness of our relation to God. It follows that the essence of the church is its inner spirit, not its sacramental relationships. Yet Martineau was a Churchman all his life. He cherished his pastorates and devoted his career to training ministers. He spoke frequently at ordinations, inductions, church dedications, and anniversaries, always addressing the importance of the Church as an institution. Martineau wanted a national church, but one based on a broad tolerance of doctrine, one that would gather those devoted to understanding the message of the gospels, and the person of Jesus, and seeking to translate those ideas into their own lives.

For Martineau, the Church is a Christian community, and in joining it one becomes part of a holy society. Its ministry should be Christian, too. As previously mentioned, Martineau opposed the entry into the Unitarian ministry of a man who, though a theist, was not a Christian.[79] The very word "Church," he said, belongs to Christianity and "was born with Christian literature, and finds its meaning exclusively in Christian institutions."[80] A church, said Martineau, is a distinctively Christian institution; Church-history is the history of organized Christianity.

Martineau acknowledged that the trust deeds[81] of his own group, the Protestant Dissenting Churches, were extremely liberal, but even they define a Christian church: "the forms of expression employed invariably assumed discipleship to Christ and kept within the limits of a Gospel exegesis."[82] For Martineau, Christ is not merely the human focus of a human organization. At the heart of Martineau's doctrine of the Church was his belief that the Christian faith required recognition of something supernatural in the life of Christ. The term "Christian" refers to those who think Christ was an original source of truth and goodness, who see in him something supernatural or divine. That, said Martineau, is what makes one a disciple instead of a fellow-pupil.[83] The divinity of Christ was not to be found primarily in his works, but rather in his person—not what Christ did but who he was. As we have seen, for Martineau, Christ's teachings were important but subordinate to his nature.

The Church, said Martineau, is an earthly fellowship with a historic continuity, a community that descends from earlier generations going back to Jesus and extends to a community in heaven. Martineau had a strong sense of the historical nature of the Church. He believed Christians owed a debt to the inheritance from the past and had an obligation to respect it and pass it on, enhanced by our effort, to those who follow.

The concept of the Church was always important to Martineau, but even more so in his later years. Waller pointed out that Martineau's hymnal of 1840, *Hymns for the Christian Church and Home*, contained only six hymns in two small sections on the Church. In the 1876 hymnal, *Hymns of Praise and Prayer*, more than 100 titles appear under the heading "The Church."[84]

The Church, said Martineau, is "[a] Society for realising harmony or reconciliation between Man and God,"[85] "an association for realising the Christian life, creating the Christian mind, and guarding from deterioration the pure type of Christian perfection,"[86] and the center of the Church is Christ.

Martineau also considered how Unitarianism related to his ideas. The Unitarians stressed free inquiry, but Martineau insisted that the Church must be more than simply an association for free inquiry. Waller wrote:

> Martineau's doctrine of the Church was not concerned simply with the individual and his relation to God, facilitated through Jesus Christ, but also with the Church as a corporate body. . . . He did have a strong sense of the Christian community; and he criticised extreme individualism which he felt undermined the corporate nature of the Church. He argued from a theological basis, and from a practical point of view, against individualism.[87]

The Church, said Martineau, is a fellowship or union that exists in order to bring people to God using the appeal and example of Christ.

Martineau also argued for the need for corporate worship: "If there is one modern tendency more than another against which I have striven through life, with the united earnestness of natural instinct and deliberate conviction, it is the extreme Individualism which turns our foremost politics, philosophy, religion, into a humiliating caricature."[88] Individualism, said Martineau, approaches anarchy. Worshippers must have a common bond, a consensus of purpose to unite them, and Martineau wanted such a common purpose to be broad enough to join all religious people. He believed in an undogmatic Church based on allegiance to Christian pieties: "The Church is the Society of those who seek harmony with God; and all who agree on the terms of that harmony, so as to seek it the same way, belong to the same Church."[89] Such a church would welcome all who seek harmony with God. "But," he asked, "would such a church be Christian? . . . If by 'Christian' you mean imbued with Christ's spirit, teaching his religion, worshipping his God and Father, and accepting his law of self-sacrifice, this would be the very essence of such a church."[90]

Thus Martineau had a broad view of Christianity, devoid of specific doctrines and requiring only the wish to be a disciple of Christ—that is, a believer in the ideas of Christ. He envisioned a united national Christian church on that basis, which would include all who wished to call themselves Christian. The national Church would appeal not to doctrines, which are only partial, transitory insights into truth, but rather to shared memories and thoughts, a heritage and tradition of desires, sympathies, and love. It would accept a congregation's own statement of its Christian purpose "on the plain principle that whoever claims the Christian name can be cast out from it by no other disciple."[91] To unite under the Christian label would commit people to the piety Jesus espoused, he said, because they would support and encourage each other. Thus it would open to them "the richest historic deposit with which Providence has blessed the world."[92] Those congregations that thought such slender doctrinal grounds inadequate could define them more strictly for themselves. He thought that all the denominations and the Church of England should pool their assets, including endowments, buildings, and treasures, to be placed in the care of ecclesiastical trustees. He did recognize that not everyone would wish to join such an organization, but that was his vision for a national Church. Martineau's upbringing and ministerial career had taught him the advantages of a Presbyterian form of government. Each Presbyterian church was bound by a covenant enacted to protect members' free interpretation of the Bible and truth from whatever source they might find it. Churches were bound to one another by affection, but they were not bound by the doctrines of a governing body. That form of church government provided services and oversight for the churches without a ruling hierarchy and gave structure without controlling doctrine. In contrast, Martineau believed, the congregational form of government was weak in that there was generally less agreement on the purpose of the church, its goals and methods of arriving at truth.

Martineau was concerned that churches spent so much effort on disputes over doctrine and the meaning of Scripture, and on opposing each other–all of which distracted them from their primary aim. For Martineau, the purpose of the church is to advance the Christian life, to bring us "into harmony with the image of Christ's mind: in our worship, looking up through it to God; in our efforts of will, lifting ever nearer to it both ourselves and the world."[93] The Church is devoted to worship and service of God, "the simple and spiritual principle of Christian communion—worship of God as disciples of Christ."[94] Martineau believed most people went to church out of devotion, not to study theology or listen to lectures. They went to church "to prostrate their souls before the Maker and Ruler of us all; to quicken their consciences for the duties of life; to see light in the troubles and sorrows of life, or to find patience under them; and to lift an infinite aspiration toward the mysterious future that awaits us all."[95]

Martineau conducted his own ministry accordingly. We build and care for churches, he said, to conform ourselves to the will of God, to devote our lives to the pattern in Heaven. The Church is the beloved community. Its special care is for the lonely, those who grieve and are sorrowful. So much in daily life divides us and separates heart from heart, said Martineau, that it is as if we are shut into individual cells. But in the church we are all one, and in looking for nourishment from the Infinite Father, the sorrows of life are put aside as we stretch forth "the hand to touch but the hem of the all-healing robe."[96] So the church brings the soul and God into intimate communion, and the secular world is shut out as we yield ourselves to the holy. Martineau believed the church should encourage the humble spirit, rather than the ostentation he found so common. The church ought to be guided by a minister who consoles and heals the sorrows of people, comforts them in their frailties, encourages their timid aspirations, leads them through prayer to a renewed understanding of their place as children of God, and helps them shed all pretense and vain pride. Martineau had enormous sympathy and understanding for the troubles people experienced, and he saw the minister's place in healing them.

B. The Church as Community

Martineau believed the church was first of all a worshipping community, whose ends were to be attained through lofty and pure worship. The church, he said, represents the visible kingdom of God on earth, and the minister is God's emissary charged with the task of bringing humanity and God together. Martineau, though, was not a strong institutionalist. Despite his grand vision of a national church, he did not seek to subordinate individual churches to a governing body. Rather, he wanted autonomy in the local organization, as he believed denominations tended to usurp the prerogatives of the local group by stressing conformity to a set of rules.

Martineau recognized the role of ministers in consoling and healing, but he disliked much of what the priestly function represented. He stressed the prophetic over the priestly office and felt that churches with strong priestly functions generally had indifferent preachers. In fact, he said, the priestly role reduces the worship leader to the level of a mechanic: "In a sacerdotal system, personal qualities go for nothing, or sink to non-essentials; whoever can administer the sacraments, can dispense God's grace; and, so long as that condition is safe, a traffic in benefices which may put a blockhead at the altar is held to involve no fatal sin."[97] The minister may seek to combine the priestly and prophetic roles, but they often conflict, and the prophetic then is lost.

In spite of such sentiments, which he reiterated many times, Martineau did fill the priestly role, though not in the sacramental sense. Most of his sermons were pastoral and dealt with the tragedies, griefs, and sorrows that are the common lot. He ministered well to his congregations and inspired them when their spirits were low, when life threatened to crush them. His moving prayers have already been discussed.

Martineau believed the prophetic office was more important than the priestly, yet he had an unusual view of prophecy. Never did he urge any social action from his pulpit. Never did he promote any organization or instruct people about civic duty. Taking Jesus as his example, Martineau believed the function of the prophet was to show people that the meeting place of God and human nature lies within them. He wanted worship to show them how to consecrate their lives. Prayers and hymns direct our thoughts to God, not to reject human potential but to remind us of our true home, which is Heaven. For all he decried the priesthood, Martineau still argued that both functions are necessary, though the prophetic ought to be stressed more:

> The Priest is the representative of men before God; commissioned on behalf of human nature to intercede with the divine. He bears a message upwards, from earth to heaven; his people being below, his influence above. He takes the fears of the weak, and the cries of the perishing, and sets them with availing supplication before Him that is able to help. He takes the sins and remorse of the guilty, and leaves them with expatiating tribute at the feet of the averted Deity.[98]

Worship at its best brings the holiness of God into the souls of men. It brings the purity of heaven into the congregation to make life divine. In Martineau's thinking, ministers do not interpose themselves between God and humanity; they narrow the distance between them.

The tension Martineau felt between the priestly and prophetic roles is a common one in the ministry. To what extent are ministers healers and consolers, and to what extent do they try to correct the ills of their people? Martineau wavered between one emphasis and the other; although he exercised both functions, this tension was always there. The young Martineau saw worship as a lonely undertaking: the individual is alone in prayers and hymns, absorbed in an inward life of wonder, sorrow, and aspiration. Later in life, however, Martineau came to understand the communal aspect of worship: "I am more aware than I was of the need of fellowship in the spiritual life, and less disposed to trust its pure spontaneity."[99] He noted that common worship makes a chorus of those who feel alone; our faith is strengthened when we overhear each other's prayers. People gathering for worship, said Martineau, reinforce each other's determination.

The variety in worship appeals to the different moods of individual congregants and encourages people to gather for a holy purpose. Although people come to worship with a variety of needs and moods, somehow there must be unity. The entire worship, with its differing elements, can, if well formed, lead the worshiper to a sense of the holy. When they sing the hymns and pray together, listen to the wisdom of the Scripture, attend the advice of the sermon, and then contribute their own spirits, toil, and talent, they prepare themselves to receive the benediction, which is the imparting of grace. Thus is the church a holy place, and the congregation a holy people.

The church, said Martineau, is subject to many needs and can be distracted by external influences, especially by the growing challenges of science and social problems. The growth of human knowledge, helpful as it generally is, has its pitfalls. Martineau saw threats to worship from many trends, such as Darwinism and positivism:

> Nor has the human conceit produced a more deplorable burlesque of faith and worship, than the scientific gospel of physiological self-interest, when preached as the whole duty of man. . . . [T]he mere fact that the human heart instinctively cries aloud for leave to worship and to trust, yet cannot do so without an outer and a higher being, irresistibly postulates the personal and living God.[100]

Thus, said Martineau, science and its progeny fascinate us, and there is a regrettable tendency to believe that the methods of science should be applied to the church—to believe that the truth must be demonstrated, tested, and known through the senses. This rule, suitable in science, does not apply to religion, Martineau believed.

Martineau spoke out against many other threats to human welfare in his day: an increasingly materialistic culture that distracts the spirit; a new faith that technology and industry can solve our most important problems; and the resulting temptation to squander our energies and talents in trifles and gadgets. The need for the Church, he said, is all the greater, and it must have the finest minds to prepare for the challenges before it in order to redeem humankind, to remind them of their immortal destiny and their obligation to the divinity within them.

C. The Decline of Christianity after the Apostles

As we have seen, Martineau saw many failings in the churches: their attempts at political power, their appeal to the upper classes, their difficulties in grappling with the many distractions that society puts before people. These problems were ancient, not unique to the industrial age. Martineau believed that Christianity had declined since the Apostolic days, that it had distorted the teachings of Jesus and had become encumbered with doctrines and creeds. These changes, Martineau said, had occurred early in the history of Christianity, and he found much in the synoptic gospels that he considered alien to the thought of Jesus. He thought, for example, that Jesus had the Messianic expectations shared by the Jews of his time but could not have uttered the apocalyptic sayings attributed to him in the gospels,[101] such as the prediction of the destruction of the Temple, the warning against false Christs who will arise, and this prediction:

> But in those days, after that tribulation, the sun will be darkened, and the moon will not give its light, and the stars will be falling from heaven, and the powers in the heavens will be shaken. And then they will see the Son of man coming in clouds with great power and glory. And then he will send out the angels, and gather his elect from the four winds, from the ends of the earth to the ends of heaven.[102]

Such sayings, said Martineau, spoke of events that had not yet happened, and the tenets of higher criticism argued against them. Further, they were out of character with the other teachings of Jesus. As previously discussed, Martineau claimed that Christianity actually negated what Christ hoped to do when it dwelt on theology about him instead of heeding his teachings directly. Martineau found the episode in Luke 9:21, in which Jesus "charged and commanded them to tell this [that he was the Christ] to no one," highly significant, as it revealed that Jesus wanted the emphasis to be on his ideas, not on his person. Martineau said:

> If the disciples had only kept that injunction instead of spending their lives reversing it, Christendom, I am tempted to think, might have possessed a purer record of genuine revelation, instead of a mixed text of divine truth and false apocalypse. For, the first deforming mask, the first robe of hopeless disguise, under which the real personality of Jesus of Nazareth disappeared from sight, were placed upon him by this very doctrine which was not to go forth,—that he was the Messiah. It has corrupted the interpretation of the Old Testament, and degraded the sublimest religious literature of the ancient world into a book of magic and a tissue of riddles.[103]

The decline of Christianity, said Martineau, came about naturally. When Jesus left them, the disciples sought to fill the gap he had left. They had expected Christ to return, but when he did not, they said that a force called the Holy Spirit had come instead. They overcame their grief at his death by proclaiming that he had risen. These two doctrines of the Holy Spirit and the Atoning Cross gave the disciples strength to carry on the work of preparing a divine society for Jesus' return.

These developments led to the formation of the church, a group devoted to remembering and carrying on the work of Jesus. Martineau noted that the New Testament records some disagreement within the Church on who should be counted as a believer—a disagreement that has persisted. Jesus had said that those are his brothers and sisters who do the will of the Father, that is, who perform neighborly deeds of compassion. But after Jesus' death, the disciples said: Jesus' ministry began with baptism, so let converts be baptized; it closed with the Last Supper, so let them take communion. Those sacraments, said the disciples, are the keys to receiving the Holy Spirit and sharing Christ's immortality. Here, said

Martineau, "in this small germ, we have the origin of that ritual and sacerdotal development of Christianity which, at every characteristic point, is a simple reversal of the Religion of Jesus, and, wherever it exists, does but wield his power to destroy his work."[104] For Martineau, church members are those who wish to be, who are devoted to the person and teachings of Christ and wish to become, with him, fully one with God.

Martineau believed that no church in Christendom was faithful to the original message of Jesus: "The spirit of Christianity has undergone decomposition."[105] He concluded with pain and dismay that Christianity had turned away from the permanent in Christ's teachings to the perishable and transient, to "what is unhistorical in its traditions, mythological in its preconceptions, and misapprehended in the oracles of its prophets. From the fable of Eden to the imagination of the last trumpet, the whole story of the Divine order of the world is dislocated and deformed."[106]

Martineau called for Christians to exalt the personal religion of Jesus over these perishable elements of Christian theology. He excoriated the doctrines of original sin, with its consignment to unmerited Hell, and the Incarnation, with its denial of the divine relation between God and all people; the doctrine of the two natures of Christ; the belief that grace is transmitted through material elements; and the apocalyptic prediction of the second coming of Christ to separate the sheep from the goats in a general judgment. Such ideas, he said, "all are the growth of a mythical literature, or Messianic dreams, or Pharisaic theology, or sacramental superstition, or popular apotheosis."[107] These extraneous doctrines, said Martineau, dilute what Jesus stood for and distort his message. Although Martineau did not object to adding to the legacy of Jesus, he thought it should be done in such a way as to preserve the integrity of the original.

D. What Is a Christian?

If the church is the combined body of Christians, what does it mean to be a Christian? For Martineau, the essence of being a Christian is following where Christ led. That involves weeding through the theological trappings about Jesus' person and returning to the original sense of his teachings. Martineau was not optimistic about the prospects for success, but he did not believe the task was hopeless.[108] Being a Christian, he said, essentially means following the two commandments of Jesus to love God and to love humankind. Accordingly, Martineau sought to replace creeds with the beatitudes, the doctrine of atonement with that of self-sacrifice, and the doctrine of the incarnation of God in Christ with that of the incarnation of God in humanity.

Martineau believed his doctrine of the incarnation in all people to be the core of religion and the primary focus of worship. God, he said, is incarnated in us in our conscience, and our duty is to obey that faculty. "All religion," he said, "is Christian in proportion as it takes up into its very substance this law of conscience, and resolves itself into a consecration of Duty."[109] Martineau cherished the demands of duty but believed them to be a consequence of religion, not a substitute for it. Christianity, he said, is more than an ethical system, and religion is more than morality: "Shall we say that the man who commits no fraud, or violence, or excess, is forthwith a denizen of the Kingdom of Heaven? God forbid! as soon might we say that every scribbler who makes no slip in scanning his metres and tuning his rhymes is a great Poet."[110]

It should be noted, however, that Martineau's attitude toward Christianity became more open-minded through the years. In his preface to the third edition of *The Rationale of Religious Enquiry*, he noted:

> There is, however, one opinion maintained in the preface to the second edition [1836], and omitted in this [1845], which it would be disingenuous to pass without a word. The name Christian is there denied to the class of persons usually called Antisupernaturalists; and for that denial reasons are given which the Author does not now think to be conclusive in their whole extent.[111]

By "Antisupernaturalists," Martineau meant those who reject a meaningful concept of God, such as Deists and Positivists. Later in life, Martineau abandoned the sweeping generalization that such people could not be Christians. Throughout his career, however, Martineau always emphasized the importance of duty to the Christian life. He believed the existence of a moral law (one aspect of God's will, although not the only one) made it that much more important for people to follow the prescriptions of God. One of the great contributions of Christianity, he said, was that it had embedded the principle of the innate equality of all people within the human heart—that it created a religious duty to work for equality.[112] That has produced the spectacle unique to Christian times of one class helping to uplift another. In Christian society, said Martineau, people work to alleviate the suffering of the miserable and the oppressed. It has been a distinct contribution of Christianity to extend benefits to all people, of whatever class or religion, and to value people according to the goodness of their hearts rather than what creeds or doctrines they recite. All of that is part of being a Christian as the term would have been meaningful to Jesus. Christians, said Martineau, also recognize the intellectual and moral nature of all humanity: we are all capable of thought and emotion because we all have a spiritual relation to the Father. Therefore are we equal before God.

Christianity, said Martineau, teaches us that we are part of something eternal. Martineau noted that Christ himself was at first a follower of John, who proclaimed a fresh order of human life at one with the future: the Kingdom of God is at hand and is already working within us. John and then Jesus invited people to join the band who awaited that kingdom. Thus did Jesus extend the bonds of fellowship beyond what John envisioned. John had invited people to come to him to be baptized in the Jordan; Jesus expanded that ministry by going out to people, rather than asking them to come to him, and by requiring only a pure heart, not baptism or any other rite.

Like John, said Martineau, Jesus believed in the coming reign of righteousness, but his methods of spreading the message were different from John's. John used the rite of baptism to initiate people who came to him. Jesus went directly to the villagers and dealt with every sort of people. He challenged people to act as God required; he baptized no one. The change from a stationary to an itinerant mission was an important precursor of the spread of Christianity. Even more important, as seen above, was Jesus' shift in emphasis from the rite of baptism to the requirement of goodness, of expunging from ourselves whatever is selfish, malignant, and depraved.

For Martineau, a Christian was not simply anyone who did good. He once defined the "characteristics of Christianity" thus:

> See then in complete array, the five wise Spirits of the soul that must stand through the night of the Bridegroom's tarrying, with their ever-constant lights of Endeavour, Humiliation, Trust, Service, and Communion. . . . I might with equal truth have called them the characteristics of Christianity, and have evoked them by appeal to Scripture, and the analysis of Christian history.[113]

He gave a stricter definition in his sermons "Historical Elements of the Christian Faith"[114] and "Christ's Definition of Neighbour."[115] There, he defined Christianity in historical terms, still avoiding a close theological definition: to be a Christian means following the religion of Jesus, "by which he reveals the living and ever living filial relation of the soul to God, and its ultimate self-harmony by absolute self-sacrifice."[116]

Elsewhere, as previously noted, Martineau outlined three articles of faith that he believed necessary for one to be called a Christian. The first article of faith is belief in the historical personality of Jesus. Faith must point to something real, but Martineau made clear that he did not require assent to any description about the capacity in which Jesus came. Second, we must acknowledge Jesus as the highest form of human sanctity and wisdom. That rule does not require considering Jesus perfect or infallible. It also recognizes him as shaped by his own family and culture. Third, "Christian faith requires the recognition of something supernatural in the life or soul of Christ; something that passeth all our understanding."[117] This something supernatural also meant that Jesus had brought a new beginning of divine light to the human conscience.

Thus, as we have seen, Martineau displayed ambivalence about what it meant to be a Christian. He worked to define what it meant to be a Christian, aware that a definition that is too broad loses its meaning. Yet—to cite one example—although he first rejected the supernaturalists, he later sought to include them. What, then, was his conclusion on the meaning of Christianity?

E. Martineau's Understanding of Christianity

Martineau was devoted to the church and sought to define it in clear terms. Christianity, in a sense, is larger than the church, certainly than the visible church. How did Martineau view Christianity? He always considered himself a follower of Christ; his criticisms of Christian orthodoxy did not reduce his veneration for Christ himself. As Drummond and Upton write, although he was accused of "destructive criticism," Martineau's "aim was always to destroy the lower in order to preserve the higher, and by a just historical method to clear away the accretions which obscured or distorted that grand and unique personality."[118]

Martineau's wish to return to the religion of Jesus did not mean, however, that he automatically preferred primitive Christianity. Just because it is older, he said, does not mean it is better:

> The representation often made of the early church as having only truth, and feeling only love, and living in simple sanctity, is contradicted by every page of the Christian records. The Epistles are entirely occupied in driving back guilt and passion, or in correcting errors of belief; nor is it always possible to approve of the temper in which they perform the one task, or to assent to the methods by which they attempt the other.[119]

Instead of being guided by the records of the early Church, said Martineau, we must strive to understand both what Jesus believed and his method of projecting his ideas. Jesus perfected in himself the image of the divine. From Jesus we derive our understanding of God, said Martineau in the response at his ordination:

> To this infinite Being, and to Him alone, do I ascribe every conceivable perfection. He is the source of power, to whom all things are possible—He is boundless in wisdom, from whom no secrets can be hidden—He is love; the origin of all good, himself the greatest; and the dispenser of suffering only that we may be partakers of his holiness—He is spotless in holiness; his will the only source of morality, and the eternal enemy of sin—He is self-existent and immutable, for ever pervading and directing all things, and searching all hearts; the Being from

whom we came, and from whom, in happiness or woe, all men must spend eternity.

From these views I infer that it is my first office, as a Minister of Christ, to awaken the attention of my people to the claims of this one infinite Jehovah upon their adoration, obedience and love.[120]

The most prominent promise of Christianity was immortality, a concept that included both the Kingdom of God in the broad sense but also personal immortality. While most Christians subscribed to this concept as an article of faith, Martineau sought to give it a philosophical basis.

5. The Hope of Immortality

Immortality, the extension of human life into eternity, lends an urgency to worship, said Martineau, because it means that worship has a lasting import. Martineau believed that idealism and the moral law implied not only eternal life, but also reward and punishment after death. Worship, then, reminds people that their beliefs, character, and conduct have far-reaching consequences for themselves and for other people, both those with us now and those who are to succeed us.

A. The Meaning of Death

Martineau believed this life to be the prelude to another, and that the manner of our lives now determines the nature of our future existence. Martineau believed that our existence on earth would be incomplete without a further existence: "Human Life has always been and will always be of indefinite duration, the time between the earthly body's birth and death being but the prologue to the real drama."[121] Further, he argued that it was logical to believe in life after death—that our very curiosity about God and the purpose of life implied that our search for understanding would not prove futile. He wrote:

> This therefore naturally leads us to consider our present state as only the dawn or beginning of our existence, as a state of

> preparation or probation for further advancement. . . . And whoever attentively considers the constitution of human nature, particularly the desires and passions of men, which appear greatly superior to their present objects, will easily be persuaded that man was designed for higher views than of this life.[122]

Martineau expounded his views on immortality in many sermons and funeral services; he was in his best pastoral form when talking about death and immortality. He expressed deeply felt sentiments to comfort his parishioners and help them confront what he believed must lie beyond. Death, he said, was first of all a transition, a migration that fulfills our destiny in another context: "Death, interpret it as you may, is at least a change of scene, a dropped organism, an entrance upon fresh conditions of being."[123] Elsewhere, he said:

> In a season of mortality, it is surely impossible to forget the relations of other scenes to this; that departure from this life is birth into another; that the immortal rises where the mortal falls; that the farewell into the vale below is followed by greetings on the hills above; so that, if sympathy with mourners here permit, the sorrows of the bereaved on earth are the festival of the redeemed in heaven.[124]

Death is the departure of the spirit that has finished its struggle, a passage to Heaven, "where are the abodes of the happy pious . . . and its companion Jesus, and its illumination God."[125] He urged the bereaved to take comfort: "As friend after friend is taken from our side we are the less detained by the world we cannot keep, and gain the clearer view of that to which we tend. The pathway of ascent to the everlasting hills is stripped of its desolation by the footprints of our forerunners, who stand already at the summit, where our life is hid with Christ and God."[126]

Although he did not dwell much on reward and punishment in the afterlife, Martineau did describe its nature. He believed death would be more than simply a migration of the spirit in some ethereal condition; it would also be a reunion with others we loved. Death, he said, "under the Christian aspect, is but God's method of colonization; the transition from this mother-country of our race to the fairer and newer world of our emigration."[127] He believed that personality would continue beyond death. Yet there remained a mystery in immortality: "we can say perhaps with a deeper quiet respecting the departed, 'We rest assured that they live; but where they live we cannot tell.'"[128]

B. The Nature of Immortality

Martineau did not believe in bodily resurrection. His Anglican friend Alexander Craufurd suggested to him that Jesus must have been resurrected because only that could explain why the disciples suddenly became joyous after Jesus' death. But, writes Craufurd, "My friend replied that he did not at all believe in any such appearances. He thought that no such abrupt transition ever occurred; he thought that it had only been imagined by Christians in later years."[129]

If not bodily resurrection, then what? Martineau believed that the wicked expected death to be the beginning of a time of punishment; the good understood it as a happy rebirth. To the wicked, death is like the exile of Prometheus on a rock in the darkest night; to the other it is "a welcome to the loving homes of the blest, amid the sunshine of the everlasting hill."[130] Many lack faith in immortality, said Martineau, because people give so much attention to their animal nature at the expense of of the mind, which alone survives.[131]

Belief in an afterlife was common among the Unitarians of Martineau's time. But Martineau differed from other Unitarians in his belief that the afterlife involved punishment. Otherwise, he said, the moral law would not extend to the next world but would stop with death. Death was not necessarily "clear from the chill of any penal shadow."[132] He said that to believe in the absence of reward and punishment in the afterlife "is a false & dangerous extreme; that it is but the softening of faith which precedes its final melting away; that the cloud which hides the abyss of Hell must inevitably rise & spread till it blots out the heaven; & that the true rescue of Christianity from the corrupting idolatry of Strength & Love must be sought in a return to the religion of Conscience."[133] We have the liberty to do right or wrong, said Martineau, but what if our behavior had no lasting consequences? Then life would be meaningless:

> And when the experiment is over, are the actors dismissed, the curtain dropped, and the theatre closed? Such an issue would contradict the very essence of moral freedom, which surely loses all significance if no difference is to be made between those who use it well and those who misuse it. When the two possible ways are thrown open to human choice, it is already anticipated that not all will take the same and provision must be made for treating those who do as they like otherwise than those who do as they ought.... [W]herever Conscience is, there we stand only in the forecourt of existence; and a Moral world cannot be final unless it is everlasting.[134]

That is, if we are all treated the same in death, then our deeds have no lasting consequences, and conscience has no abiding value. We can live for the moment, said Martineau, or for eternity. The one who lives for the moment is alienated from God; the other passes into a condition of grace. Martineau said that many are torn between those two urges, and

> For those who cannot take the whole distance at a bound, God has prepared, between the natural and the spiritual, the heroisms, the martyrdoms, the sanctities, of History. If we cannot live at once and alone with him, we may at least live with those who have lived with him; and find, in our admiring love for their purity, their truth, their goodness, an intercession with his pity on our behalf.[135]

Thus, says Martineau, God gives us role models. But, he adds, we must also serve as role models for others. We do not understand how far-reaching our influence may be, he said; in our lifetime, we affect people around us and even people we do not know; but our influence also continues beyond this life. The noble nature, he says, is aware of its immortality and knows that the spirit will walk "in dignity within the paradise of God's Eternity."[136] Doubts result from our animal nature: selfishness, ignorance, and grossness cast a veil over our destiny after death.

C. The Assurance of Immortality

When Craufurd asked Martineau whether he ever had doubts about immortality, Martineau replied, "I cannot say that I am entirely free from them; but they are only transient."[137] Martineau's belief in immortality was intuitive. We have an innate sense, he claimed, that there is more than this present life provides. If justice exists in the governance of the universe, then immortality is necessary: "if Death gives final discharge alike to the sinner and the saint, we are warranted in saying that Conscience has told more lies than it has ever called to their account."[138] It would make no sense, he said, if the thirst for God were in vain, if goodness and nobility had no lasting consequences.

Christianity, said Martineau, assures us that our soul will continue to exist: "The Soul of Christ, the sinless, risen, and immortal, is the pattern shown to us."[139] We feel this in our hearts and in our worship as we become committed members of the church, which is the allegorical body of Christ. In the end, Martineau's belief in immortality rested on his faith in God, and his sermons and other writings contain many eloquent passages to that effect. For example, he writes: "God would never launch so frail a vessel on so stormy a sea, where the roll of every wave may wreck us, were it not designed to float at length on serener waters, and beneath gentler skies. O God! It is terrible to think what may be lost in one human life; what hope, what joy, what goodness, may drop with one creature into the grave!"[140]

Another passage on immortality is worth quoting at length because of its persuasive beauty and eloquence of argument for belief in a moral God:

> If the celestial hope be a delusion, we plainly see who are the mistaken. Not the mean and grovelling souls, who never reached to so great a thought; not the drowsy and easy natures, who are content with the sleep of sense through life, and the sleep of darkness ever after; not the selfish and pinched of conscience, of small thought and smaller love; no, these in such case are right, and the universe is on their miserable scale. The deceived are the great and holy, whom all men, aye, these very insignificants themselves, revere: the men who have lived for

something better than their happiness, and spent themselves in the race, or fallen at the altar of human good; —Paul, with his mighty and conquering courage; yes, Christ himself, who vainly sobbed his spirit to rest on his Father's imaginary love, and without result commended his soul to the Being whom he fancied himself to reveal. The self-sacrifice of Calvary was but a tragic and barren mistake; for Heaven disowns the godlike prophet of Nazareth and takes part with those who scoffed at him and would have him die.[141]

D. Future Salvation

Martineau's understanding of salvation encompassed the hope of redemption in the next world. Martineau did not believe in the vicarious atonement, nor did he believe that salvation could be achieved by rites or by subscription to any doctrine or creed. The belief that our sins have been expunged by another violated his sense of morality; he believed that we must each bear our own responsibility, that we must be neither condemned for what another has done nor saved by the deeds of another. So if Adam ate of the fruit of the tree of knowledge, that does not condemn anyone else:

> When a sentence is proclaimed against crime, is it indifferent to judicial truth, upon whom it falls? . . . Is this the sense in which God is no respecter of persons? Oh! what deplorable reflection of human artifice is this, that Heaven is too veracious to abandon its proclamation of menace against transgressors; yet is content to vent it on goodness the most perfect [i.e., Jesus]. No darker deed can be imagined, than is thus ascribed to the Source of all perfection, under the insulted names of truth and holiness.[142]

Martineau's ideas about salvation relate closely to his belief about immortality. We live eternally, Martineau believed, but in what condition? For what may we hope after this life? In his view, salvation depends on our present lives. Ironically, he noted, there are two types of people who never worry about salvation. First are those that devote themselves to selfish aims and mean desires, who never aim as high as salvation, being slaves to their grosser nature. Second are those that are inspired by lofty ideals and noble goals,

> that are occupied by the secret conceptions of character which their life is a perpetual but unlaboured attempt to embody; that do gentle and generous deeds because there is nothing else in their imagination; that do battle for truth and rectitude, because it is the only spirit of combat in their hearts; that bear up against suffering nobly because they discern in every trial more purifying love than grief.[143]

Of such people, he wrote: "Salvation hereafter, like happiness here, is best secured by those who do not incessantly strive after it."[144]

Salvation is attained by heeding the dictates of conscience, by conforming one's self to the summons of the divine within, earnestly striving after the example Jesus set, and cultivating the excellence of character that results from obedience to the moral law. Martineau believed that guilt and sin are real, and he argued that Unitarians had been falsely accused of believing that God overlooks our guilt. In fact, he said, most Unitarians agreed with him that "No guilt is overlooked until it is eradicated from the soul."[145] Such guilt may indeed be eradicated by a change of heart. Although deeds cannot be undone, there can be repentance and atonement. Yet achieving salvation was not easy, as Martineau said in one of his prayers:

> Why, then, O Father, everpresent, are we so unlike to thee, and quite unworthy to be called thy children? We have wasted the hours thou hast trusted to our care and served the appetites thou has given us to rule. We have not learned the heavenly wisdom by which the yoke of life becomes easy and its severest burden light; but are still chafed by restless cares, depressed by light sorrows, and provoked by trivial infirmities.[146]

For Martineau, our purpose—indeed, the meaning of salvation—was oneness with the Infinite God. "While we are on one side of nature," he wrote, "the Infinite God is on the other. . . ."[147] We approach God through our devotion, by offering up our best selves. Martineau believed that service to and love of other people will not necessarily help us to love God, but the love of God in any true sense will lead us to express our love to other people, who are endowed equally with us as children of God, the object of God's benediction, and sharers of God's immortality. Salvation comes, then, through our union with God.

As we have seen, Martineau's theology was complex, and he strove for internal consistency in his elaboration of what he saw as the Christian message. Among the finest of the Dissenting thinkers, his particular genius was to explain theology in terms of philosophy and to reconcile their criticisms of each other. Martineau laid the ground for strong belief in a personal God that dwells in all people, not just in Jesus. His doctrine of human nature showed a keen understanding of people, their problems, dreams, and their needs, and the way in which they can find God. And Martineau sought to recover the authentic Jesus and show his importance to us. Martineau's doctrine of the church and the promise of immortality provided a well-rounded theology.

Notes

1. "Absolute Mind" is a term used by the German Idealists to express the concept of God in philosophical terms.
2. *Essays II*, 346.
3. *Essays IV*, 98.
4. *The Seat of Authority in Religion*, 305.
5. *Ibid.*, 302–3.
6. "What Is Christianity? No. 7: True Idea of a Revelation, No. 2," 1.
7. *Essays IV*, 247.
8. *Essays IV*, 516.
9. *Essays III*, 6.
10. *The Seat of Authority in Religion*, 14.
11. *Hours II*, 158.
12. *Essays IV*, 179.
13. *Essays IV*, 588.
14. *Endeavours*, 503.
15. *Hours II*, 77.
16. *Essays IV*, 426.
17. *Essays III*, 169; italics in original. The portion in quotation marks is Poynting's original text.

18. *Endeavours*, 352.
19. *Essays III*, 147.
20. *The Seat of Authority in Religion*, 29.
21. *Ibid.*, 304.
22. *Hours II*, 4.
23. Preface to *Ten Lectures on the Positive Aspects of Unitarian Thought and Doctrine*, xiii.
24. *Hours I*, 83.
25. "The Faith of Suffering," 9.
26. *Endeavours*, 187.
27. *Hours II*, 26.
28. *Essays III*, 170.
29. *Hours II*, 108.
30. *Hours I*, 247.
31. "What is Christianity? No. 6: True Idea of a Revelation, No. 1," 2.
32. *Hours I*, 341.
33. *Hours II*, 66.
34. *Essays IV*, 14.
35. Letter to the Rev. V. D. Davis, August 13, 1894, quoted in Drummond and Upton II, 212–13.
36. *Hours I*, 14.
37. *Hours II*, 289.
38. Carpenter, 176.
39. "Christian View of Moral Evil," *The Liverpool Controversy*, 4.
40. *Endeavours*, 20.
41. *Endeavours*, p. 471.
42. *Ibid.*
43. *Hours I*, 232.
44. *Endeavours*, 377.
45. *Endeavours*, 370.
46. *Endeavours*, 358–59.
47. "Spirit of Christianity, No. 5: Providence, No. 1," 4.
48. "The Faith of Suffering," 4.
49. *Ibid.*, 5.
50. *Essays II*, 74.
51. Socinianism is characterized by the belief that Christ is our saviour because of his teachings and exemplary life. Socinians saw Jesus as a man given divine power through the resurrection. Adherents stressed the importance of faith—trust in God and in Christ—as essential for salvation. Humanity, they said, is mortal by nature, and immortality is a gift of God. They believed in the authority of the Bible and claimed that God is known only through Scriptural revelation, not through natural theology. Only the righteous, they said, will be resurrected; sinners will suffer eternal extinction.
52. "Christ's Conception of Human Nature," 1.

53. *Hours II*, 225.
54. *Hours II*, 352.
55. "Christ's Conception of Human Nature," 1.
56. Waller, *James Martineau*, 178.
57. *Essays IV*, 456.
58. Waller, *James Martineau*, 166.
59. *Hours I*, 192.
60. *Studies of Christianity*, xix–xx.
61. *Essays IV*, 477–78.
62. Drummond (1908), 298. Drummond himself, disagreed, arguing that the word translated "Lord" [kurios] was in the time of Jesus a title of respect, often used in addressing a stranger, as in John 12.21, where Philip is accosted as "Lord."
63. *National Duties*, 211.
64. *Hours II*, 203.
65. *Ibid.*, 203–4.
66. *Hours II*, 208–9.
67. Matthew 5.48.
68. *Hours I*, 73.
69. *The Seat of Authority*, 356–61.
70. "Spirit of Christianity, No. 5: Providence, No. 1," 9.
71. *The Seat of Authority in Religion*, 575.
72. "Appendix" to "Loss or Gain in Recent Theology," 16–17.
73. *The Seat of Authority in Religion*, 328.
74. *Studies*, 193.
75. "Spirit of Christianity, No. 5: Providence, No. 1," 11.
76. "The Negative Faith," 9.
77. "What is Christianity? No. 6: True Idea of a Revelation, No. 1," 5.
78. *Essays IV*, 7.
79. Letter to V. D. Davis, HMC MS Davis 1:88, March 29, 1897. The candidate was Charles Voysey, who had been an Anglican cleric. After rejection for the Unitarian ministry, Voysey formed his own theistic church in Langham Place, London.
80. HMC MS Davis 1:84.
81. In Martineau's day, each church drew up a Deed of Trust, similar to modern church constitutions, stating the terms on which members gathered and what ideas would bind them.
82. HMC MS Davis 1:86–87.
83. *The Rationale of Religious Enquiry*, vii.
84. Waller, *James Martineau*, 267.
85. *Essays II*, 388–89.
86. *Essays IV*, 447.
87. Waller, *James Martineau*, 209.

88. *Essays II*, 404.
89. Quoted in Drummond and Upton I, 418–19.
90. *Ibid.*
91. From "Letters on 'Open Trusts,'" July 1882, quoted in Drummond and Upton II, 101.
92. *Essays II*, 520.
93. *Essays IV*, 441.
94. Letter to the Rev. Edwad Talbot, September 21, 1866, MNC MS 5:18.
95. "Address by The Rev. James Martineau, delivered at The Soiree held in the Hope Street School-Room, Liverpool, September 25, 1871," 2.
96. *Essays IV*, 18.
97. *Essays IV*, 350.
98. "Christianity Without Priest and Without Ritual," 37–38.
99. *Home Prayers*, vii.
100. *Hours II*, 7–8.
101. See also the contribution of Timothée Colani as described in Schweitzer, 224f.
102. Mark 13.24–27.
103. *The Seat of Authority in Religion*, 329.
104. *Ibid.*, 515.
105. "The Demand of the Present Age for an Enlightened Christian Ministry," 37.
106. *The Seat of Authority in Religion*, 649–50.
107. *Ibid.*, 650.
108. *Essays II,* 521.
109. *Essays IV*, 448.
110. *Ibid.*, 449–50.
111. *The Rationale of Religious Enquiry*, vii.
112. *The Rationale of Religious Enquiry*, 96.
113. *Essays IV,* 466.
114. *National Duties*, 206–18.
115. *National Duties*, 184–85.
116. *National Duties*, 218.
117. *Ibid.*
118. Drummond and Upton I, 210.
119. *Essays IV*, 475.
120. "Address at the Ordination of the Rev. James Martineau to the Co-Pastoral Office over the Congregation of Eustace-Street, Dublin, February 13, 1829," 26.
121. Preface to *Ten Lectures on the Positive Aspects of Human Thought and Doctrine*, xiii.
122. *A Study of Religion* II, 352.
123. *Hours II*, 146.
124. *Endeavours*, 196.
125. *National Duties*, 365.
126. *National Duties*, 369.

127. *Endeavours*, 457.
128. *A Study of Religion* II, 345.
129. Craufurd, 145–46.
130. *Studies*, 197.
131. *Endeavours*, 291.
132. "The Doctrine of Punishment," 4.
133. *Ibid.*
134. *A Study of Religion* II, 360–61.
135. *Hours I*, 239.
136. *Endeavours*, 299.
137. Craufurd, 156–57.
138. *A Study of Religion*, 365.
139. "The Service at Hope Street Church, Liverpool, on Thursday, December 31, 1863, on occasion of The Induction of the Rev. Alexander Gordon, B.A., One of the Ministers of the Church," 20.
140. *Endeavours*, 295.
141. *Endeavours*, 133–34.
142. "The Scheme of Vicarious Redemption Inconsistent With Itself," 17–18.
143. *National Duties*, 128–29.
144. *Ibid.*, 128.
145. "The Scheme of Vicarious Redemption," 20.
146. *Home Prayers*, 54–55.
147. *Hours I*, 53.

Chapter VI: Conclusion

This book has sought to elucidate Martineau's views on worship and the beliefs that undergirded them. Martineau's key contributions to worship lay in the realms of theology, philosophy, and church practice. In theology, he promoted new doctrines of human nature, foremost among them his belief that God incarnates himself in people. In philosophy, he argued that the conscience was far more than a learned faculty, shaped by culture—that it was in fact the presence and voice of God within us. He proposed a strong doctrine of human nature: with Jesus, we incarnate God, and worship aims to develop in us our awareness of that divine presence. In church practice, he showed that worship could combine the highest sentiments and affections with a strong theoretical structure, uniting art with tradition and beauty of expression.

For Martineau, worship is intended to connect people with the ultimate and permanent, that which is God within ourselves. As we have seen, his service as a pastor to three churches and as a teacher and principal at Manchester College gave him a solid experiential foundation for his theories about Unitarian worship and ecclesiology. We have seen how Martineau's concept of worship was theoretically grounded in a theology that directed people to the divine incarnate God within them. The promise of God within was fulfilled in Jesus, as it can be for us. For Martineau, the primary significance of Jesus was an example of humanity at its highest, evidence of what we all might become as we strive for union with God.

Worship is a means of access to God, and Martineau believed in the possibility of access to God without intermediaries. The Bible (written as it was by fallible humans) and the example of Christ, he said, show us what we might be, but they cannot replace our reliance on the God within.

As we have seen, the question of authority was critical for Martineau. Early in his career he claimed that reason was the highest authority; later, he argued that in fact conscience, the voice of God within us, is the greatest authority. He examined a variety of common sources of authority—reason, the Bible, tradition, and the moral law—and decided that, valuable as each was, they did not reach to the core of religion. Therefore he turned to conscience, and the more he examined the idea, the more convinced he became that our conscience is not merely God speaking to us, but the voice of God within us speaking–an important distinction.

Another key point in Martineau's theology was his understanding of what it meant to be a Christian. For Martineau, it simply meant following where Christ led. We do not worship Christ; with Christ, we worship the Father. Martineau saw in Jesus the most nearly complete revelation of God, and an example of the highest of human possibilities.

We have seen that Martineau, although a Unitarian, considered himself first and foremost a Christian. He helped Unitarianism to deepen its understanding of Christian tradition. Further, he disliked sectarianism and urged the churches to use the title "Free Christian Church" instead of any denominational label. Many of the Unitarian churches in England today still use that term.

Martineau sought to weaken the Unitarian reliance on Scripture as a source of authority, replacing it with conscience, as the voice of God, guided by reason. And he sought harmony between reason and faith. In the words of Henry Gow, by the early 20th century, "Unitarianism, largely under the influence of Martineau, was no longer a religion dependent upon Biblical authority. It was a religion of the free Spirit controlled by Reason and Conscience. It held fast to the great affirmations of Christianity. It believed in God and the soul. It regarded the teachings of Jesus as the Way of Life, and the life of Jesus as the highest ideal of manhood."[1]

Notes

1. Gow (1928), 130.

Bibliography

Abbreviations

Endeavours *Endeavours After the Christian Life: Discourses*
Hours I *Hours of Thought on Sacred Things: A Volume of Sermons*
Hours II *Hours of Thought on Sacred Things: Second Series*
National Duties *National Duties and Other Sermons and Addresses*
Studies *Studies of Christianity: Or, Timely Thoughts for Religious Thinkers. A Series of Papers*
Essays I, II, III, or IV *Essays, Reviews and Addresses*

Note: Where no city of publication is noted, London is to be assumed.

1. Works by Martineau
A. Manuscripts and Letters

The letters and manuscripts of Martineau are catalogued in Harris Manchester College Library; works cited without publication information may be found there. The most easily accessible collection of Martineau's letters is in James C. Drummond and C. B. Upton, *Life and Letters of James Martineau*, 2 vols. (1905).

To V. D. Davis, June 10, 1897, MS Davis 4:42–43; also MS Davis 1:1–91, October 4, 1878–December 12, 1897; MS Davis 1:34–35, April 15, 1886; Davis 1:90–91, December 12, 1897

To R. B. Darbishire, February 2, 1857, MS MNC 4:30
To Martineau from Samuel Kell, February 5, 1857, MS MNC 4:34
To William Gaskell, September 14, 1857, MS MNC 5:261–63
To Edward Talbot, September 21, 1866, MS Martineau 5:17–18.

The following sermons are in manuscript, transcribed from Martineau's shorthand notes by his daughter, Gertrude Martineau, in 1906. They are all located in Harris Manchester Library, MS HMC Martineau, J 18-i and 18-ii. The manuscripts are not numbered individually. The dates indicate when Martineau gave the sermon. Where two dates are given, they represent the first and last dates he preached the sermon.

"Christening Address" (1850–1871)
"Christ's Conception of Human Nature" (March 24, 1849–December 19, 1870)
"The Doctrine of Punishment" (February 6, 1848–November 13, 1870)
"The Faith of Suffering" (November 24, 1850–May 1, 1870)
"The Negative Faith" (January 25, 1846–October 15, 1871)
"Nature and God" (November 15, 1849–December 5, 1852)
"The Religion of Conscience & the Religion of Love" (April 5, 1835–January 4, 1857)
"Spirit of Christianity, No. 5: Providence, No. 1" (April 21, 1844–March 25, 1866)
"St. Paul's Doctrine of the Church and the Sacraments" (April 4, 1841–June 21, 1863)
"Testimony of Christianity to the power of Human Affections" (December 25, 1836–December 25, 1871)
"The Two Directions of Mediatorial Theology, and Transylvanian Appeal" (May 10, 1847, October 15, 1865, and October 17, 1869)
"Valedictory Address" (June 25, 1885)
"What is Christianity? No. 6: True Idea of a Revelation, No. 1" (February 6, 1842–December 15, 1870)
"What is Christianity? No. 7: True Idea of a Revelation, No. 2" (February 20, 1844–January 29, 1871)
"What is Christianity? No. 8: Relation of Scripture History to Christianity, No. 1" (March 6, 1842–November 10, 1844)
"What is Christianity? No. 11: Relation of Belief to Character" (May 1, 1843–February 12, 1871)
"What is Christianity? No. 12: Spirit of Christianity, No. 1" (February 18, 1844–December 17, 1870)

B. Printed Sermons

Again, dates indicate when Martineau gave the sermon. Where two dates are given, they represent the first and last dates he preached the sermon.

"Address on Induction of a New Minister," in National Duties; reprinted 1864 in Bolton
"The Besetting God," in *Endeavours*
"The Better Part," in *Hours I*
"The Bible and the Child," in *Essays IV*; delivered at Paradise Street Chapel, Liverpool, July 1845
"Charge to Minister and Congregation," in *Essays IV*; delivered at the Induction of the Rev. Alexander Gordon, Hope Street Church, Liverpool, December 31, 1863
"The Child That Needs No Conversion," in *Hours II*
"The Child's Thought," in *Endeavours*
"Christ, the Divine Word—I," in *Hours II*
"Christ, the Divine Word—II," In *Hours II*
"Christening Address I," in *National Duties* (1856)
"Christian Doctrine of Merit," in *Endeavours*
"Christian Self-Consciousness," in *Endeavours*
"The Christian Student," in *Essays IV*; delivered at Opening of Session, Manchester New College, London, October 1856
"The Claims of Christian Enterprise," in *Faith and Self-Surrender*
"Communion Address—I," in *Hours II*
"Communion Address at the Opening of Manchester College Thursday, October 19, 1893," in *Proceedings and Addresses on the Occasion of the Opening of the College Buildings and Dedication of the Chapel, October 18–19, 1893*
"The Communion of Saints," in *Endeavours*
"Confirmation Address," in *Hours II*
"Confirmation Address—II," in *Hours II*
"The Contentment of Sorrow," in *Endeavours*
"The Darkened Heart," in *Hours II*
"The Discipline of Darkness," in *Hours I*
"Divine Justice and Pardon Reconciled," in *Hours I*
"Eden and Gethsemane," in *Endeavours*
"Faith the Deliverance from Fear," in *Hours II*

"Faith the Root of Knowledge and of Love," in *Faith and Self-Surrender*
"The Family in Heaven and Earth," in *Endeavours*
"The Finite and the Infinite in Human Nature," in *Hours I*
"Five Points of Christian Faith," in *Studies* (1841)
"Forgiveness to Love," in *Hours I*
"The Free-Man of Christ," in *Endeavours*
"The God of the Living," in *Essays IV*; delivered at the Opening of Oakfield Road Church, Clifton, November 10, 1864
"The Godly Man," in *Hours I*
"The Good Soldier of Jesus Christ," in *Endeavours*
"The Goodness Which May Be Taught," in *Hours II*
"Great Hopes for Great Souls," in *Endeavours*
"The Ground of National Unity—I," in *National Duties* (1854, 1866)
"The Ground of National Unity—II," in *National Duties* (1854, 1865)
"Having, Doing, and Being," in *Endeavours*
"Help Thou Mine Unbelief," in *Endeavours*
"His Eye Seeth Every Precious Thing," in *Hours II*
"How Sayest Thou, 'Shew us the Father?'" in *Hours II*
"Ideal Substitutes for God," in *Essays IV*
"Immortality," in *Endeavours*
"In Him We Live and Move and Have Our Being," in *Hours II*
"Influence of the Doctrine of a Millennium," in *National Duties* (1838, 1868)
"The Inner and Outer Kingdom of God," in *Hours I*
"The Kingdom of God Within Us, Part I," in *Endeavours*
"The Kingdom of God Within Us, Part II," in *Endeavours*
"The Lapse of Time and the Law of Obligation," in *Faith and Self-Surrender*
"Life According to the Pattern in the Heavens," in *Essays IV* (1854)
"Life to the Children of the Prophets," in *Hours I*
"Limits of Divine and Human Forgiveness," in *Hours II*
"Lo! God is Here!" in *Endeavours*
"Looking Up, and Lifting Up," in *Endeavours*
"Mammon-Worship," in *Endeavours*
"The Messenger of Change," in *Hours I*
"The Moral Quality of Faith," in *Hours I*
"The Mutual Duties of Nations," in *National Duties* (1854, 1866)
"Need of Culture for the Christian Ministry," in *Essays IV*; delivered at Cross Street Chapel, anniversary of Manchester New College, January 24, 1835
"Neither Man nor Woman in Christ Jesus," in *Hours I*

"Nothing Human Ever Dies," in *Endeavours*

"Obedience and Communion," in *Hours II*

"The Offering of Art to Worship," in *Hours II*

"The Outer and the Inner Temple," in *Essays IV*; delivered at the opening of Upper Brook Street Chapel, Manchester, September 1, 1839.

"The Outer and Inner World," in *The Essex Hall Pulpit*, vol. 1 no. 1, January 1893

"Parting Words," in *Essays IV*; delivered on the completion of his ministry of 25 years at Hope Street Church, Liverpool, August 2, 1857

"Pause and Retrospect," in *Essays IV*; delivered on leaving Hope Street Church for a year's travel and study, July 16, 1848

"Peace in Division: The Duties of Christians in an Age of Controversy," in *Studies*

"Perfection Divine and Human," in *Hours I*

"The Place of Man in the Scale of Life," in *Hours II*; note: incorrectly listed in the table of contents as "How Much is a Man Better than a Sheep" (his text)

"Plea for Biblical Studies and Something More," in *Essays IV*; delivered at Opening of Session, Manchester New College, London, October 1858

"The Powers of Love," in *Hours I*

"The Prayer of Faith," in *Hours II*

"The Relation Between Ethics and Religion," in *Essays IV*; delivered at Opening of Session, Manchester New College, London, October 1881

"Religion as Affected by Modern Materialism," in *Essays IV*; delivered at Opening of Session, Manchester New College, London, October 1874

"Religion in Parable," in *Hours I*

"Religion on False Pretences," in *Endeavours*

"Rest in the Lord," in *Hours I*

"Scope of Mental and Moral Philosophy," in *Essays IV*; delivered at Opening of Manchester New College at Manchester, October 1840

"Secret Trust," in *Hours I*

"Seek First the Kingdom of God—II," in *Hours I*

"Self-Surrender to God," in *Hours II*

"A Sermon," delivered at the induction of the Rev. Alexander Gordon, B.A., as a minister of Hope Street Church, Liverpool, December 31, 1863; published in pamphlet form

The Service at Hope Street Church, Liverpool, on Thursday, December 31, 1863, on occasion of The Induction of the Rev. Alexander Gordon, B.A., One of the Ministers of the Church (1864), in *Essays IV* "The Seven Sleepers," in *Endeavours*

"Silence and Meditation," in *Endeavours*
"The Single and the Evil Eye," in *Endeavours*
"Sorrow No Sin," in *Endeavours*
"The Soul's Forecast of Retribution," in *Hours II*
"The Sphere of Silence II," in *Endeavours*
"The Spirit of Life in Jesus Christ," in *Endeavours*
"The Spirit of Trust," in *Hours II*
"The Spiritual Charity of Christendom," in *Hours II*
"The Strength of the Lonely," in *Endeavours*
"Temptations of Power," in *Hours II*
"That the Christ Ought to Suffer," in *Hours II*
"Theology in its Relation to Progressive Knowledge," in *Theology and Piety Alike Free*
"Thou Art My Hiding-place," in *Hours II*
"Thou Art My Strength," in *Faith and Self-Surrender*
"Three Stages of Unitarian Theology," in *Essays IV*; delivered at the anniversary of the British and Foreign Unitarian Association, May 19, 1869, at Unity Church, Islington
"The Tides of the Spirit," in *Hours I*
"Time, to Nature, God, and the Soul," in *Hours I*
"The Transient and the Real in Life," in *Hours II*
"The Unclouded Heart," in *Endeavours*
"The Unknown Paths," in *Hours I*
"The Unjust Steward," in *National Duties* (1837, 1870)
"Valedictory Address I," in *National Duties*
"Valedictory Address II," in *National Duties* (1875)
"Valedictory Address III," in *National Duties* (1877)
"Valedictory Address V," in *National Duties* (1879)
"Valedictory Address VI," in *National Duties* (1880)
"Valedictory Address VIII," in *National Duties* (1883)
"Views of the World from Halley's Comet," in *Essays IV*; delivered at Paradise Street Chapel, Liverpool, September 27, 1835
"The Watch-Night Lamps," in *Essays IV*; delivered on the first Sunday of public worship in Hope Street Church, Liverpool, October 21, 1840
"The Way of Remembrance," in *Hours II*
"Why Dissent?" in *Essays IV*; delivered at Opening of Session, Manchester New College, London, October 1871
"Winter Worship," in *Endeavours*

"The Witness of God with Our Spirit," in *Hours I*

"A Word for Scientific Theology," in *Essays IV*; delivered at Opening of Session, Manchester New College, London, October 1868

"Worship in the Spirit," in *Essays IV*; delivered at the opening of Rosslyn Hill Chapel, Hempstead, June 5, 1862

C. Lectures, Essays, and Addresses

"Address at the Interment, On Occasion of the Death of the Rev. Robert Brook Aspland, M.A." (1869)

"Address at the Ordination of the Rev. James Martineau to the Co-Pastoral Office over the Congregation of Eustace-Street, Dublin," February 13, 1829.

"Address by The Rev. James Martineau, delivered at The Soiree held in the Hope Street School-Room, Liverpool, September 25, 1871," Cross Street Chapel, Manchester, October 21, 1871 (Abbreviated and altered version of "The Church of the Future. A Speech Delivered by The Rev. James Martineau at the Hope-Street School Rooms, Liverpool, on Monday, September 25, 1871.")

"Address, On Occasion of Laying the Foundation Stone of a New Church in Hope Street," Tuesday, May 9, 1848, in *Essays IV*

"Address, Presented to James Martineau, D.D., LL.D., On his Eighty-third Birthday, April 21, 1888, and Dr. Martineau's Reply; with A List of Signatures"

"Appendix," published anonymously as a reply to the address "Loss or Gain in Recent Theology," by the Rev. Dr. Allon, President of the Congregational Union of England and Wales, on its Autumnal Meeting in Manchester on October 4, 1881

"The Ascension," in *National Duties* (1840, 1870)

"The Battle of the Churches," in *Essays II*

"The Bible: What It Is, and What It Is Not; A Lecture delivered in Paradise Street Chapel, Liverpool, on Tuesday, February 19, 1839," in *The Liverpool Controversy*

"Characteristics of the Christian Theory of God," in *National Duties* (1837, 1868)

"Christian View of Moral Evil. A Lecture, Delivered in Paradise Street Chapel, Liverpool, on Tuesday, April 30, 1839" [part of the "Liverpool Controversy"]

"Christianity Without Priest and Without Ritual," in *The Liverpool Controversy*
"Christ's Definition of 'Neighbour,'" in *National Duties* (1836, 1870)
"The Church of England," in *Essays II*
"The Church of the Future, a Speech Delivered by the Rev. James Martineau, at the Hope-Street School-Rooms, Liverpool, on Monday, September 25, 1871"
"Church-Life? Or Sect-Life? A Second Letter to the Rev. S. F. MacDonald, in Reply to the Critics of the First," in *Essays II*
"The Crisis of Faith," in *Essays II*
"The Demand of the Present Age for an Enlightened Christian Ministry," in "Two Discourses, The Former by John Kenrick, M.A., The Latter by James Martineau, Delivered in Cross-Street Chapel, Manchester, January 24, 1836, in commemoration of the Fiftieth Anniversary of the Foundation of Manchester College" (1836)
"Factors of Spiritual Growth in Modern Society," in *Essays IV*
"Faith in Christ for His Own Sake," in *National Duties* (1840, 1870)
"Francis William Newman; 1. Phases of Faith," (1850) in *Essays III*
"Francis William Newman; 2. New Passages in 2nd Edition," (1853) in *Essays III*
"Funeral Address—I," in *National Duties* (1833)
"Funeral Address—II," in *National Duties* (1858)
"The God of Revelation His Own Interpreter," in *Essays IV*
"Historical Elements of the Christian Faith," in *National Duties* (1842, 1868)
"Report of Proceedings at a Special General Meeting of the Congregation of Hope Street Church, held on Sunday, 22nd February, and, by adjournment, on 8th March 1857"
"Introductory Chapter," in John James Tayler, A *Retrospect on the Religious Life of England, or, The Church, Puritanism, and Free Inquiry* (1876, 2nd ed.)
"A Letter, Addressed to the Dissenting Congregation of Eustace-Street, [Dublin] by the Rev. James Martineau, upon his declining to receive the Royal Bounty" (1832)
"Loss and Gain in Recent Theology," in *Essays IV*
"Memoir and Papers of Dr. Channing," in *Essays I*
"Memorial Preface," in John Hamilton Thom, *A Spiritual Faith*
"Mind in Nature and Intuition in Man," in *Essays IV*
"Modern Materialism: Its Attitude Towards Theology. A Critique and Defence," in *Essays IV*
"Moral Influence of Reliance Upon Faith," in *National Duties* (1873, 1869)
"The National Church as a Federal Union," in *Essays II*

"Nature and God," in *Essays III*
"New Affinities of Faith, A Plea for Free Christian Union," in *Essays II*
"Presentation to the Reverend James Martineau, June 1872"
"Proceedings in Connection with the Resignation of The Rev. James Martineau, Christmas, 1872 (Little Portland Street Chapel, London)"
"Professional Religion," in *Essays II*
"The Proposition 'That Christ is God,' Proved to be False from the Jewish and Christian Scriptures. A Lecture Delivered in Paradise Street Chapel, Liverpool, on Tuesday, March 12, 1839," in *The Liverpool Controversy*
"Prosperity to Manchester College" [toast at luncheon on the opening of Manchester College, Oxford, Thursday, October 19, 1893], in *Manchester College, Oxford. Proceedings and Addresses on the Occasion of the Opening of the College Buildings and Dedication of the Chapel, October 18–19, 1893* (1894)
"Religion as Defined by Modern Materialism," in *Essays IV*
"The Religion of Assurance and the Religion of Desire," in *National Duties* (1836, 1869)
"Report of Proceedings at a Special General Meeting of the Congregation of Hope Street Church, held on Sunday, 22nd February, and, by adjournment, on the 8th March, 1857"
"The Scheme of Vicarious Redemption Inconsistent With Itself and The Christian Idea of Salvation. A Lecture, Delivered in Paradise Street Chapel, Liverpool, on Tuesday, March 19, 1839" [part of the "Liverpool Controversy"]
"Speech" [delivered at the meeting of the Trustees of the College, held in University Hall, June 24, 1886, in support of a resolution], in *Theology and Piety Alike Free*
"The Sphere and Spirit of Faith," in *National Duties* (1845, 1868)
"Suggestions on Church Organisation: Being an Address Delivered by The Rev. Dr. Martineau, at the National Conference Held at Leeds, April, 1888"
"The Transient and the Permanent in Theology," in *Essays II*
"Theodore Parker," in *Essays I*
"Tracts for Priests and People," in *Essays II*
"The Unitarian Position, A Letter Addressed to the Rev. S. F. MacDonald" (1859)
"A Way Out of the Trinitarian Controversy," in *Essays II*

D. Books

Biographical Memoranda, in Waller, Ph.D. Thesis, Appendix A
A Collection of Hymns for Christian Worship (Dublin, 1831)
Common Prayer for Christian Worship: in Ten Services for Morning and Evening, with Special Collects, Prayers, and Occasional Services (1871)
Endeavours After The Christian Life: Discourses (9th ed., 1892)
Essays, Reviews, and Addresses (1891)
    Vol. I: Personal: Political
    Vol. II: Ecclesiastical: Historical
    Vol. III: Theological: Philosophical
    Vol. IV: Academical: Religious
Faith and Self-Surrender (1897)
Home Prayers, With Two Services for Public Worship (1891)
Hours of Thought on Sacred Things, A Volume of Sermons (1876)
Hours of Thought on Sacred Things. Second Series (Boston, 1880)
Hymns for the Christian Church and Home, Collected and Edited by James Martineau (5th ed., 1846)
Hymns of Praise and Prayer, Collected and Edited by James Martineau, LL.D. (1874)
In Memoriam John Kenrick (1878, printed for private circulation)
National Duties and Other Sermons and Addresses (1903)
Prayers In the Congregation and in College (1911)
The Rationale of Religious Enquiry, or, The Question Stated of Reason, The Bible, and the Church; in Six Lectures (3rd ed., 1845)
The Seat of Authority in Religion, Third Edition Revised (1891)
Studies of Christianity: Or, Timely Thoughts for Religious Thinkers. A Series of Papers, ed. William R. Alger (Boston, 1858)
A Study of Religion, Its Sources and Contents (2 vols., Oxford, 1888)
Types of Ethical Theory (2 vols., 1885)
Unitarianism Defended: A Series of Lectures by Three Protestant Dissenting Ministers of Liverpool: In Reply To A Course of Lectures, Entitled, "Unitarianism Confuted," by Thirteen Clergymen of The Church of England, by James Martineau, the Rev. John Hamilton Thom, and the Rev. Henry Giles (Liverpool and London, 1839)

2. Secondary Sources

Armstrong, Richard A., ed., *Discourses by the late Charles John Perry, B.A., Delivered in Hope Street Church, Liverpool, With a Memoir by the Editor, and a Funeral Sermon by Prof. J. Estlin Carpenter, B.A.* (Liverpool, 1884)

Armstrong, Richard A., *Martineau's "Study of Religion": An Analysis and Appreciation* (1900)

Brown, Andrew, *James Martineau (1805–1900): The Development of His Religious Thought and its Influence on 19th Century Unitarianism as Reflected in His Editorship of His Three Hymn Books* (Harris Manchester College, March 1998)

———, *Index of James Martineau's Hymn Books* (Harris Manchester College, 1998)

Bousset, Wilhelm, *Kyrios Christos*, tr. John E. Steely (Nashville, TN, 1970)

Burkitt, F. C., *Christian Worship* (Cambridge, UK, 1930)

Carpenter, Joseph Estlin, *James Martineau, Theologian and Teacher, A Study of His Life and Thought* (1905)

Cashdollar, Charles D., *The Transformation of Theology, 1830–1890: Positivism and Protestant Thought in Britain and America* (Princeton, NJ, 1989)

Chadwick, John W., *James Martineau, A Sermon* (1900)

Chadwick, Owen, *The Victorian Church*, 2 vols. (1966, 1970)

Channing, William Ellery, *The Works of William Ellery Channing, D.D.* (Boston, 1890). See especially his sermons "Unitarian Christianity" (1819), "Unitarian Christianity Most Favorable to Piety" (1826), "Christian Worship" (1836), and "The Church" (1841).

Channing, William Henry, *The Life of William Ellery Channing, D.D.* (Boston, 1904)

Chryssides, George D., "The Seat of Authority in Unitarianism," in *Diskus* vol. 4 no. 1 (1996)

Clark, Henry W., *History of English Non-Conformity*, 2 vols. (1913)

Collyer, Rev. Robert, *James Martineau* (1900)

Craufurd, Rev. Alexander H., *Recollections of James Martineau, With Some Letters from Him and an Essay on His Religion* (Edinburgh, 1903)

Darbishire, R. D., ed., *Theology and Piety Alike Free: From the Point of View of Manchester New College, Oxford. A Contribution to its Effort Offered by an Old Student*, ed. (1890)

Davies, Horton, *Worship and Theology in England from Newman to Martineau, 1850–1900* (1962)

Davies, J. G., *A Dictionary of Liturgy & Worship* (1972)

Davis, V. D., ed., *A Minister of God, Selections from the Occasional Sermons and Addresses of John Hamilton Thom*; edited with a Memoir by V. D. Davis (1901)
———, *A History of Manchester College* (1932)
Drummond, James, and C. B. Upton, *Life and Letters of James Martineau*, 2 vols. (1905)
Drummond, James, *Pauline Meditations* (1919)
———, *Studies in Christian Doctrine* (1908)
Emerson, Ralph Waldo, "Compensation," in *Essays, First Series* (Boston, 1896)
———, "Self-Reliance," in *Essays, First Series* (Boston, 1896)
———, "The Transcendentalist," in *Nature, Addresses, and Lectures* (Boston, 1895)
The Essex Hall Hymnal Revised (1902)
Freckelton, T. W., *Religion in Modern Thought* (1893)
Gordon, Alexander, *Heads of English Unitarian History* (1895)
Gow, Henry, *The Unitarians* (1928)
Hall, Alfred, *James Martineau, The Story of His Life* (1906)
Hastings, James, ed., *Encyclopedia of Religion and Ethics* (Edinburgh, 1914)
Herford, Brook, *The Story of Religion in England* (1908)
Howland, C. H., ed., *James Martineau, Passages from his Writings, Selected by C. H. Howland* (Chicago, IL, circa 1886)
Hymns of the Spirit for use in the Churches of the Free Spirit (Boston, 1937)
In Memoriam James Martineau 1805–1900. Supplement to *The Inquirer*, 20 January 1900. (Pages are not numbered; those given are supplied by the author, counting from the title page as page one.)
Jacks, Lawrence P., "Authority in Religious Belief," in T. W. Freckelton et al., *Religion in Modern Thought* (1893)
Jackson, A. W., *James Martineau, A Biography and Study* (Boston, 1900)
Jones, Henry, *The Philosophy of Martineau in Relation to the Idealism of the Present Day* (1905)
Julian, John, D. D., ed., *A Dictionary of Hymnology, Setting Forth the Origin and History of Christian Hymns of All Ages and Nations* (1907)
Lee, Sidney, ed., *Dictionary of National Biography*, Supplemental Vol. III (1901)
Lewis, H. D., "The British Idealists," in Ninian Smart, ed., *Nineteenth Century Thought in the West*, vol. 2 (Cambridge, UK, 1985)
Livingston, James C., "British Agnosticism," in Ninian Smart, ed., *Nineteenth Century Thought in the West*, vol. 2 (Cambridge, UK, 1985)
Lloyd, Walter, *Protestant Dissent and English Unitarianism* (1899)
Macquarrie, John, ed., *Contemporary Religious Thinkers from Idealist Metaphysicians to*

Existential Theologians (1968)

McLachlan, Herbert, *The Unitarian Movement and the Religious Life of England* (1934)

Mellone, Sydney Herbert, *Leaders in Religious Thought in the Nineteenth Century* (1902)

Ould, Fielding, "The Practical Importance of the Controversy with Unitarians," in *Unitarianism Confuted* (Liverpool, 1900)

Parker, Theodore, *A Discourse on Matters Pertaining to Religion*, vol. 1 of *Complete Works* (Boston, 1907)

Pfleiderer, Otto, *Philosophy and Development of Religion*, 2 vols. (Edinburgh, 1894)

Presentation to The Reverend James Martineau, June 1872 [pamphlet]

Priestley, Joseph, *A History of the Corruptions of Christianity*, 2 vols. (Birmingham, 1782)

Pulbrook, Martin, "The Light of the World (An Alternative Christmas Story)," in *The Inquirer*, December 19, 1998, p. 6

Reardon, Bernard M. G., *Religious Thought in the Victorian Age: A Survey from Coleridge to Gore*, 2nd ed. (1995)

———, *Liberal Protestantism* (1968)

Roberts, H. D., *Hope Street Church Liverpool and the Allied Nonconformity* (Liverpool, 1909)

Schleiermacher, Friedrich, *On Religion, Speeches to its Cultured Despisers*, tr. John Oman (New York, 1958)

Schneewind, J. B., *Sidgwick's Ethics and Victorian Moral Philosophy* (Oxford, 1977)

Schulman, Frank, *"Blasphemous and Wicked": The Unitarian Struggle for Equality 1813–1844* (Oxford, 1997)

———, *Charles Wellbeloved: A Study of a Dissenting Minister*, B.D. dissertation, Oxford, 1997

Schweitzer, Albert, *The Quest of the Historical Jesus, A Critical Study of its Progress from Reimarus to Wrede* (1926)

Short, H. L., C. G. Bolam, Jeremy Goring, and Roger Thomas, *The English Presbyterians* (1968)

Smart, Ninian, *The Concept of Worship* (1972)

Smart, Ninian, John Clayton, Patrick Sherry, and Steven T. Katz, *Nineteenth Century Religious Thought in the West*, 3 vols. (Cambridge, UK, 1985)

Strauss, David Friedrich, *Life of Jesus Critically Examined*, 2nd ed., tr. George Eliot (1892)

Sunderland, Jabez T., *James Martineau: A Brief Sketch of His Life and Work* (Toronto, 1905)

Tayler, John James, *A Retrospect of the Religious Life of England; or, The Church, Puritanism, and Free Inquiry*, 2nd ed. (1876). See also the "Introductory Chapter" by Martineau.

Ten Lectures on the Positive Aspects of Unitarian Thought and Doctrine, delivered by various ministers, under the auspices of the British and Foreign Unitarian Association, in St. George's Hall, London, in March and April, 1881, with A Preface by Rev. James Martineau, D.D., LL.D., 3rd ed. (1881)

Thom, John Hamilton, *A Spiritual Faith* (1906)

Troeltsch, Ernst, *The Absoluteness of Christianity* (1972)

Unitarianism Confuted: A Series of Lectures Delivered in Christ Church, Liverpool, in MDCCCXXXIX. By Thirteen Clergymen of the Church of England (Liverpool, 1839)

Vogt, Von Ogden, *Art and Religion*, rev. ed. (Boston, 1948)

Wainwright, Geoffrey, ed., *The Study of Liturgy* (1978)

Waller, Ralph, *James Martineau: His Emergence as a Theologian, His Christology, and his Doctrine of the Church, with Some Unpublished Papers*, Ph.D. thesis, University of London, September 1986

———, "James Martineau: The Development of His Thought," in *Truth, Liberty, Religion: Essays Celebrating Two Hundred Years of Manchester College*, ed. Barbara Smith (Oxford, 1986)

———, "Scenes of Manchester College from the Eyes of James Martineau," in *Transactions of the Unitarian Historical Society*, April 3, 1997.

Webb, Clement C. J., *A Study of Religious Thought in England from 1850* (Oxford, 1933)

Welch, Claude, *Protestant Thought in the Nineteenth Century*, 2 vols. (New Haven, CT, 1972 [vol. 1], 1985 [vol. 2])

Wilbur, Earl Morse, *A History of Unitarianism: In Transylvania, England, and America* (Cambridge, MA, 1952)

www.ingramcontent.com/pod-product-compliance
Lightning Source LLC
Chambersburg PA
CBHW031247290426
44109CB00012B/478